PUBLISHED *by* PARABLES
Earthly Stories with a Heavenly Meaning

Change…The Inevitable
Christopher J. Taylor

Change…The Inevitable

By Christopher J. Taylor

PUBLISHED *by* PARABLES
Earthly Stories with a Heavenly Meaning

Readers should be aware that Internet Web sites offered as citations and/or sources for further information may have been changed or disappeared between the time this was written and the time it is read.

Change…The Inevitable

By Christopher J. Taylor

PUBLISHED by PARABLES
Earthly Stories with a Heavenly Meaning

Change…The Inevitable
Christopher J. Taylor

Table of Contents

Acknowledgements

First and foremost, I want to give honor and thanks to the heavenly Father, for without him, none of this would be possible. Very special thanks must be given to the matriarch of our family, Luella M. Taylor. Along with being my grandmother, she was my number one fan. No matter what mischief I found myself in, she always put her arms around me.

My mother, Karen Denise Taylor, is the smartest person I know. Her unconditional love has sustained me over these years of being institutionalized. I acknowledge my father, Joe Alfred Taylor, Sr. For through the good, bad and ugly, your consistent love is like a rock. It causes me to know that I can always count on you. I am forever grateful for your love and strength. A special love and acknowledgement goes to my two sisters, Stacy R. Cooper and Danielle A. Taylor. We grew up together, and I'm blessed to have always felt your presence. This is to my Aunt Patricia Butler. For as long as I can remember, you have been the glue that held this family together. A special note of appreciation goes to my cousins, Abdul, Omar and Ahmad.

I am so appreciative to Johneen "Aunt J" Buffard who taught me that love and loyalty make a family. It is not just being related. You have been a part of our family since I was a little boy. Because of your love each day, I can stand a little taller. A very special thank you goes to Francine Segura and her two beautiful daughters, Elicia and Faith. You let me know that it is okay to dream again and that "pain is never wasted." I thank you from the bottom of my heart. To Carol "'Tia J" Segura and Aaliyah "Baby J" Segura, as well as Scott Watson. I have been blessed by your presence and thank God for the opportunity to know you. I send special heartfelt thanks to you all for everything you have done for myself and my family.

When I think about change, I must recognize my brothers in this fight. These men have both mentored me and along-side attributing to my overall growth as person. A note of appreciation to Rory Atkins and Travis Barnes. I blessed to have a team so diverse and driven, thank you for fighting this fight with me. S.U.R.G.E.! At these gates, the S.U.R.G.E. Community is the first line of offense in our promotion for change. I thank you for stepping up to this challenge and for allowing me to serve alongside you. S.U.R.G.E. stands for "Seeking Understanding Reaching Goals Everyday". We are a team of men and women who have found a commonality amongst each other. That we have to take extreme ownership of our lives. The S.U.R.G.E. Team is committed to four core pillars. They are, 1) Repairing Citizenship 2) Redeeming space and time through the proper use of energy 3) Encouraging our community through empowerment and 4) Building better people, instead of better prisoners.

Thank You to Samuel Connally, Gene Melendez III and Stephen Futrell Jr. Thank you to William S. Graham. You've been extremely influential to me and you are an excellent example of thinking outside the box. Much love to my brothers, Rodney Marshall, Jr. Robert "Bobby" Manigo, and Robert "Lil Rob" Whitaker IV, you all have been a part of my life since childhood and have never turned your backs on me. Thank you for showing me what it means to be a friend. Special thanks to Alexander and Timira Montoya along with the entire Montoya family. It's funny how God will put people in your life at precisely the right time and place. For me, this family has been an example of love, loyalty, and acceptance. I am forever thankful for them and the way that they've put their arms around me. These men and women have redefined the way I approach life, love, and relationships. Some I've known forever, others I've met a little further down the road in my journey. None the less, God has Surrounded me with a team of beautiful people and I am forever thankful. Authentic people, show authentic love, and I'm blessed to have this family in my corner.

I salute Yasmin Salina and The Hustlers Guild. Your investment into the next generation and your innovative approach is second to none. I want to honor Monica Chambers, Maggie, Jeanie, Jenny, Keri and the whole Restorative Justice team. The work that you do enables us to heal and helps us to offer healing to those who need it most. A note of admiration goes to Dr. Ashley Hamilton, Julie Reda, and the DU PAI family. Thank you for giving so many men and women the space to be themselves, to become comfortable in their own skins, and to create. It has been a blessing being a part of this family. My gratitude goes to the Wood family, Kayla, Eric, Eli, Seton, Jonah, Claire, and Grant. Also, a Special thanks goes to the Wood family along with Mary "Mama Mary" Faimon.

Before I bring this to a close, I want to extend a notion of gratitude to Warden Ryan Long, Associate Warden Gates-Fouse, Major Todd Crist, Major Rosa Frayre, Capt. Kathy Mestas, Capt. Daniel Davis, Capt. Janesse Mitchell, Lt. Mindee Mitchell-Brown Lt. Kevin Williams, Sgt. Flowers (Sgt. S.U.R.G.E.), Kelli "Ms. E" Eagans, Rachael Badar, Marcella Hilton, Falon Lewis, Kylisha Rowland, Alysia Johnson, Ama Wobil, the entire Denver Complex nursing staff and Denver Complex management team. I thank you for allowing me an opportunity to earn the platform, to promote change and to invest into the community that I am a part of.

Preface

"Life will only change when you become more committed to your dreams than you are to your comfort zones"

- Anonymous

Life is a journey! That's true for all who have been given the opportunity to live. That being said, some of our paths have been a bit bumpier than others. For the longest time, I have trudged through what seemed like the rockiest of roads. I have often wondered, "Why do things have to be so hard?" I mean I have literally bumped my head a thousand times seemingly learning the same lesson over and over again. It wasn't until I had spent over a decade in prison, serving a life sentence, that I began to understand the errors of my thinking. For me, my life had to change in order for me to change the way I was living it.

My name is Christopher J. Taylor and it's a privilege to be able to share some of my thoughts, experiences, and observations with you in "Change...The Inevitable." What are you looking for when deciding whether or not to read a book? Some people expect credentials such as "World Renowned" and "Best Selling Author". Well, let me be the first to say, I haven't reached that status...yet. However, life has taught me a few very valuable lessons. Many of which I've had to learn the hard way.

The idea of "Change" is a universal law. At the same time, it is one of the most difficult things to accept. Learning this has shifted my perception in profound ways. It has led me down a path of self-reflection, growth, and development. It wasn't easy. For anyone looking to take things to the next level, I hope that you understand that it's not a walk in the park.

I grew up in a high crime neighborhood, and I eventually bought in to the "street life" ideology. I became a gang member at a young age, I dropped out of school, and I sold drugs. This path set me on the fast track to prison. By the age of 18, I was already headed to Carter County Detention Center in Ardmore, Ok. I was sentenced to 2 years in prison, and I served 22 months of that sentence. I had the option of going to Dallas, TX, where my mother was, or I could go back home to Denver, Co., where I had been living before going to prison. I chose to go home, and that meant that I would back in the neighborhood.

Returning to Denver, I found myself engulfed in the gang violence that had been escalating between my "gang" and a "rival gang". I had only been home for 6 weeks before my father's home had been shot up in multiple drive by shootings. One week later, I was sitting in the Arapahoe County Justice Center facing murder, attempted Murder, and assault charges. That was in 2005.

It's 2022 and needless to say, I no longer live by those faulty "street rules". These days, I've learned to live a life of service. Primarily, I work in the Denver Reception and Diagnostic Center's Infirmary as an OCA III or Offender Care Aid Level III. We aid incarcerated men with special medical needs, and with all daily living tasks. I'm a part of a team of mentors called S.U.R.G.E. (Seeking Understanding Reaching Goals Everyday) We promote the ideas and concepts of change by investing time, energy, and resources into the community that we're a part of.

Change…The Inevitable
Christopher J. Taylor

Sooner or later, we all reach a point where we become tired of the way we've been living and the results we've been getting. We reach a point where we want to do better. Unfortunately, we don't always know how to do this. This book is a comprehensive guide to understanding the roles that our past have played in creating our present, and how our present is molding our future. My aim is to shift the conversation away from justifying perspectives like "we are victims of circumstance" and "products of the ghetto" to that of a responsible person. By understanding the power in being responsible for our choices, we take a vested interest in our outcomes.

Since my 18th birthday, I've had 10 weeks of freedom. Today, I'm 36 years old. There is not a day that passes where I do not think of the people that I've hurt and the lives that I've damaged with my actions. I have learned from my poor choices and life style and it's even more important that I offer my story to the men and woman that I have an opportunity to mentor. At the same time, it's imperative that I maintain respect for Kyle Boyd, Ms. Susan Holyfield, and the life of Krystal Martinez. I do not want to cause any more pain then I already have, so that story will not be a part of this book. I will say this. For all that I've put them through, it's my commitment to the universe that I will forever live this life serving whatever community I'm a part of.

With that being said, let's get to work!

Christopher J. Taylor

This book is dedicated to the memory of

Krystal Martinez

Perception

When you hear the word perception, what's the first thought that comes to your mind? I've heard people make reference to that old philosophical question, "Is the cup half full or half empty?" According to Dictionary.com, as a noun, the definition of the word perception is:

1. **Perception**-*The act or faculty of perceiving or apprehending by means of the senses or of the mind; cognition; understanding.*

According to Merriam-Webster.com the word perceive as a verb means:

1) *A:to attain awareness or understanding of;*
   b: to become aware through the senses.

The word "perception" is a mental impression of something perceived by the senses together with comprehension of what it is. In short, it's our mental view, the way in which we see the world. Of course, we have our five (5) senses such as the sight, sound, smell, touch and taste to help filter information from the natural world. It's through these powerful tools through which we gather information; however, our mind will take that same information and process it accordingly to our own personal perspective. Let's look again at the philosophical question in light of the definitions above: is the cup half full or is it half empty?

Change...The Inevitable
Christopher J. Taylor

Let's say we have an eight-ounce glass and we fill it with four ounces of water. As you know, it will be exactly half full and half empty at the same time. Now, let's say we get one hundred people to look at this glass and ask them, "Is the cup half full or half empty?" Without using tricks, gimmicks or mirrors, something very interesting will begin to take place. A certain percentage of the people will describe the glass as being half full. The others will see it as half empty. How is it that the same group of people looking at the same glass will have a different perception of this glass of water? The answer is simple. The glass is both half-full and half-empty. However, based upon their perception, people will see things differently. Why does this happen? We've all learned how to process data, but that process is based on our individual intellectual capacity. This is determined by how, when, and where we were born and raised.

When we talk about change, we have to understand how much our perspective can dictate our behaviors. When we change, it's not just about the behavior. It's about changing the thinking that created the flawed responses in the first place. Throughout this book, we'll discuss the necessity of change and the role that our perception plays in that process. We'll challenge our thinking on multiple levels. We will take an in depth look into our past experiences, and we will gain understanding that everything that we have ever been through has played a role in shaping our outlooks and mental views. Just remember change is inevitable! Whether your change is for the better or not ...well that is going to be up to you.

Outside of death itself, change is the only other guarantee in life. Don't believe me? Just ask the dinosaurs! The entire face of our planet has changed countless times since its creation. From the simple movement of the tectonic plates to the volcanic eruptions that form rocks. Changes are constantly taking place. They are visible and invisible. They are also tangible as well as intangible. Populations Increase and decrease almost constantly through birth and death. Technology is ever evolving at such an alarming rate. The human mind can't keep up with it. One hundred and seventeen years ago, a man by the name of Henry Ford created the first automobile in 1901. Today, amidst changes and technology, not only can we drive cars. Now cars can drive and park themselves!

In 1996, Tupac died, yet we can see him in concert through the advancements in hologram technology. When I was a child, cell phones were the size of a brick with a long black antenna. Today they are literarily pocket-size computers, and they have capabilities that blow the average mind. Since the moment of our conception, we have been changing, I mean, I can't speak for anyone else, but I most definitely didn't come out of the womb 5 feet 11! So, why is it, so many of us refuse to accept this natural law? A lot of us aren't ready to change, and that's understandable, it is an uncomfortable process. However, we must understand that we are creatures of habit and that we find comfort in routine. We have to be willing to allow ourselves to be molded and stretched if we are to become who we were created to be.

Then there are people who truly desire changes. However, they haven't figured out how. Another scary thing about habits and routine is that they can have a crippling effect on our lifestyles. Have you ever known someone that had to have everything done their way or the highway? What about the infamous "I need to go on a diet" conversations, that we have with ourselves every other week? You know the one that typically pops up right after we binge on Ben and Jerry's ice cream, Grandma's cookies, and way too many bread sticks. At the core of it all, once we get into a routine, it can be an urge struggle to change things up. Of course, we can't forget about the ones who don't have any issues at all. You know the holier than thou ones, with their nose all up in the air. They are quick to tell you about all your shortcomings but you can't say anything about theirs. They are those type of people. I bet you could name a few right off the bat!

We all know someone like this. If you don't, then the odds are it's probably you! The bottom line is change is a part of life. So, you can sit back and let life happen to you, or you can make life happen for you. Do you remember the old idioms, "You can't teach an old dog new tricks" Or what about the one that states, "You can take the brotha out of the street, but you can't take the streets out of the brotha?" A lot of people hold on to these thinking errors, and they really believe that they are incapable of change. Perhaps you've heard your Grandparents say, "Don't mind Grandpa. He's just set in his ways." The fact is that we, as human beings, are designed to adapt and evolve to whatever environments we are in. Not just to maintain, but we have within our DNA the ability to evolve and thrive. The proof is in all life forms. This is seen especially in all of mankind's accomplishments from hunter gatherer to walking aboard the international Space Station. The bottom line is that we are amazing. So, who are we to say that you can't teach old dog new tricks? Our existence is the Evidence. We have to do better... we have to be better ...because we *are* better.

Progress is a process. That's the first step to understanding this journey. This is not an easy thing to do. In fact, the entire process is going to be very uncomfortable. However, our goal is to become the person that we were created to be, to operate at an optimum level, and to win! Look at the changes from a Caterpillar to a Butterfly, and from an Apple seed to an Apple tree. Look at the changes from the broken, bitter, and abused to the confident, secure, and renewed. We've been stuck, held victim by circumstances and unhealthy habits and routines. We are not victims! We are more than survivors. We are overcomers. However, in order to reach our greatest self and our finished product, we have to go through this process. What process? In the chapters to come, I'll share with you about the various stages of change.

Change…The Inevitable
Christopher J. Taylor

Chapter 1

Perspective

"There are lessons and blessings in everything that we go through"

Christopher J. Taylor

There are various types of trauma ranging from psychological to physiological, yet it all plays a part in forging and shaping our personalities and lives.

According to the online dictionary, Webster- Merriam the word Trauma is defined as:

> **Trauma** *-1a: an injury (such as a wound) to living tissue caused by an extrinsic agent b: a disordered psychic or behavioral state resulting from severe mental or emotional stress or physical injury c: an emotional upset.*

Drama-3: *a state, situation, or series of events involving interesting or intense conflict of forces.*

Let me introduce you to a typical family living anywhere in the USA. Jeff and Laura are the parents of two twin boys named Kevin and Keith. It is late and the kids are in bed. While in their beds, they suddenly are awakened by the sounds of commotion coming from the living room. Their mother, Laura, is telling her husband Jeff, "Please calm down. It's not that serious." Her husband, in a drunken state, replied, "I pay the bills here. Don't tell me what to do in my own house." He began striking her so forcefully that she fell to the floor with a bloody nose. The sound of the commotion caused the children to jump out of bed, open the door, and walk down the hall. All they can hear is their father screaming at their mother and telling her to get up off the floor and go get him another beer. She sees the boys and turns away. She gathers herself as she climbs to her feet and goes to put the twins back to bed. Suddenly, Jeff grabs her arm and strikes her again. This time, Kevin runs to his mother, and jumped in between them screaming. While Keith seemed frozen in place. Jeff releases his hold on Laura and stumbles backwards. Laura, in tears, grabs the boys and rushes them back to their room, and begins to comfort them. As she puts them back in bed, she promises that everything will be okay. Kevin is crying and Keith hasn't said much. However, it's clear that both boys have been affected by all of this. Suddenly, their father starts screaming again, "Laura!" He yells from the living room. She reassures the boys that everything will be fine one last time and leaves the room.

This is not the first domestic dispute within this family. In fact, the twins grow up in a very abusive atmosphere. Their mother was abused and they themselves experience being constantly "spanked" and "whipped". While both Kevin and Keith were raised in this environment, their shared experiences affected their individual perspectives in different ways. For Kevin, this type of abuse forged within him the disposition that he will never put his hands on a woman. The reason is that he had seen what his father did to his mother. The very thought of domestic violence gives him anxiety to the point that he can't watch a movie that depicts it without being disturbed. Keith, on the other hand, is affected in a different way. Witnessing his father beat his mother resonated with him. It is an example in which a man is supposed to treat a woman. He remembers being beaten and spanked when he did something wrong. He concludes that this is "normal," and that this is the way a person should be treated when they've done something wrong. Kevin, who grew up being both verbally and physically abused, carries those negative behaviors into his relationships particularly towards women. He follows his fathers' abusive patterns that he witnessed throughout his childhood.

This is simply cause and effect. The twins experienced a turbulent upbringing which impacted their perspectives as they matured. The purpose of the story is to shine light on the fact that we are all different. The way we experience a moment or a situation, especially when we are young, will affect our life in different ways. When we are children, our minds are like a blank canvas. As we learn and experience life, we will begin to draw upon this canvas creating a sort of map. This is one that we use as reference when we find ourselves maneuvering through life. This is a process in which we learn to filter information which ends up forming an ever-evolving picture. However, some of us find ourselves repeating the same process and ending up with the same picture. Everything we experience, whether good, bad, or indifferent. will shape the way that we think and feel about people, and the world we live in. Our perspective is formed early on, and will play a major role in our behaviors and responses.

The funny thing about trauma is that it is universal. This means that we all have to experience or will face an event that will change us. For some, it may be a scary run in with a dog. For others, it may be a car accident. None the less, those things can have a lasting effect on a person so. When we reflect on the things that we have been through, we have to pay attention to three very important things. 1) What was my behavior before the event? 2) What was the actual event? 3) How has the event changed my behavior moving forward? With all due respect, everyone is not going to be ready to go into those dark moments. I definitely understand. Life is real, and the truth is that it can seem unbearable at times. However, I want to extend to you, that we all have our own burdens to bear. Thankfully, we don't have to bear them alone. There are communities of over-comers who have come together with the intent to heal and support one another. So, as you begin to dig into the traumas of your past, be prepared to experience some old feelings, and if need be, reach out to any support groups in your area. As you're reading this, keep in mind that it's in our most uncomfortable moment. As we experience the most growth. I'm encouraging you to change your life before life changes you.

Let me ask you a question. What does the ideal you look like? How does this person handle conflict? How does this version of you view relationships? How do you think that version feels when faced with conflict? Self-image is an important part of our perception. How we see ourselves is typically how we think the world see us. An Insecure person might see a group of people looking at them. When they are laughing, they automatically assume they are laughing at them. A defensive person may take everything a coworker says as a direct insult on them. We are projecting our thoughts onto other people, and the way that we project is indicative of the way we see ourselves. The flip side of this is that we can improve our self-image, and this, in turn, improves our quality of life. After all, once I know that I'm worth more than I've been giving myself, I'll stop selling myself short.

When we start the reflection, we can begin to bring up the traumas of our past. Then we begin to address those root issues, and reshape how we see the world and the people in it. The next step in the process is the actual work. We have to learn the power of application, because if you knew better you would do better, right? You'd be surprised how many people don't. The following makes absolutely no sense at all. You spend years in college, studying for a degree, only to graduate and get a job flipping burgers. I know a lot of people who went to school, and amassed thousands of dollars in school loans. Only, they got a job in a totally different profession that they never received education for. All the while, they're working to pay off student loans. I'm not judging. I'm simply stating a fact, and to be honest it just doesn't make any sense. Once we have been informed, the next step is to become transformed. It's imperative that we take what we have learned, and apply it to the best of our ability. Since we are being honest, this is the one thing that really is easier said than done.

I remember when I was learning how to play basketball, and I mean that I was horrible. I didn't have any coordination, no real strong suit, and I didn't have the physical skill set that came from the repetition of daily practice. Nonetheless, I wanted to learn, and I wasn't going to quit until I figured it out. Needless to say, I still stink at basketball. However, I did manage to pick up a good understanding of the game.

Looking back on my life, I reflect on numerous situations where I knew better, yet still made the wrong decision like so many of us do. A lot of the times I lacked discipline, point blank. Other times I allowed myself to be influenced by peers, as well as my own insecurities. I can also remember times when I was in situations, and honestly had no real direction. I mean literally, I had no idea what the right choice was or should have been. Those moments became complete learning experiences.

When we speak about change, we have to accept that it is inevitable. Next, we have to understand that we can get ahead of the tide and change our lives. Or, we can take the reactive position and sit back while life changes us. The choice is 100% up to you. This life is 100% yours. You have the say so in how your life looks, or the way you want to live it. The sooner we understand our power, our responsibilities in our life, and that we can truly do anything that we put our mind to. Then, the sooner we will begin to walk in own divine right. I say all that to say this, "Our past made us the people that we are today." Not only that, but it also serves as a template. It is something we can always refer back to and learn from. Along with that same train of thought, I know that my past has shaped my present. The same is true in that my present will shape my future.

Change...The Inevitable
Christopher J. Taylor

Now, let's talk about a few components of life that forge our world in which we live. Drama and trauma are two words that we've heard which offend about everyone undoubtedly. They come from things that we face almost every day. From the moment we emerge from the wombs of our mothers, took our first breath of life and open our eyes to the time we close them forever—drama and its' partner trauma are with us. There are various types of trauma ranging from psychological to physiological, yet it all plays a part in forging and shaping our personalities and our lives.

The late Dr. Liala Afrika, a powerful author and holistic doctor, said "Trauma keeps you in a state where you can't do anything, especially something that requires long-term planning and execution". Another powerful prolific author, the late Dr. Edward Robinson had this to say about drama. "Drama is the sword that reaches into the subconscious, pierces that thick wall and goes down into the subconscious thus attitude. Drama changes attitude and attitude changes behavior". Just from these two powerful statements alone, there is an abundance of insight and information on the effects of trauma and drama that have been given. The explanations above shed light on the story of the twins. All of us are like Kevin and Keith in some shape, form or fashion. Remember, trauma is universal, meaning we are all affected by it. We will face events that will undoubtedly make an impact which changes us. For some, it may be a scary run in with a dog. For others, it may be a car accident, maybe family disagreements or situations with co-workers. Nonetheless, these things can have a lasting effect on a person. Keep in mind that every situation is not good, but good can come out of every situation.

Change…The Inevitable
Christopher J. Taylor

Chapter 2

Hindsight, Foresight, and Insight

"He who controls the past controls the present, and he who controls the present controls the future"

Anonymous

Hindsight

"Hindsight is 2020." Have you ever heard those words before? How about "In order to know where you are going, you have to know where you have been?" What do these sayings mean to you? When I was younger, I felt like they were real cool catch phrases, you know, someone would make a reference to a situation that they were in. (like a mistake with a girlfriend) At the time, they didn't see their fault in the break up. However, looking back on it, they were able to see where they went wrong. My response would be, "Well, you know what they say, hindsight is 2020". However, I never had a real understanding of the statement. It wasn't until I was much older that I really began to look deeper into the meanings of these different idiomatic and catchy comebacks. Let's take a deeper look at Merriam-Webster's definition of hindsight from the internet.

Hindsight *(n)-Perception of the nature of an event after it has happened.*

The above definition was simple. It was clean and straight to the point. Note the words "after it has happened..." This phrase means that while we are in a situation, we may not be able to freely comprehend the moment. However, after the fact, and through a little reflection, we can gain a clearer understanding of things.

Hindsight plays an extremely important role in breaking down experiences. It shines a light on the way those experiences have influenced our thinking. That, in turn, is the starting point to changing how we think today. It's in understanding where our faulty thinking originated.

This is a memory I have when I was nine years old. I was walking up the street in northeast Denver, and I had a basketball that I was trying to learn how to dribble. (This is something that I still struggle with today) Nonetheless, I'm walking and bouncing a ball. Then, the ball hits the tip of my foot and bounces off into a neighbor's bush. Of course, I didn't think anything of it. So, I ran in the bush after my ball. All of a sudden, I heard the sound of some very aggressive bees! Before I was able to run, I was stung three times. (once in the head, once under my arm, and once on the collar bone.) I took off running! I was screaming like the devil himself was chasing me, and I was forgetting about the basketball and everything else. I got to the house and burst through the screen door screaming. I'm crying, and my Dad thought something was really wrong with me. He jumps up grabs me and says, "What's wrong"? I started to tell him what happened, and he lets me go, sits back down and starts laughing. Now I'm confused at his reaction to my situation to the point that I stopped crying. I looked at my dad like, "What in the world is really going on with him.?" Without saying anything, he told me to go wash it off and bring the peroxide. I did what he told me to do, and while he's cleansing the area, he starts to explain why he was laughing. I recalled him asking me how many times he has told me about playing in bushes and turning over rocks. I sat and looked at him still waiting to hear what was so funny. He continued by saying "This is what I was trying to get you to look out for. You never know what could be under a rock or in bushes. There could be snakes, spiders or anything else. You have to be careful when playing outside. Nature will bite and sting you without warning."

You know how kids are. We've heard all the warnings before, right? Do we listen? No! However, it was a little different now having a feeling in memory to attach to the warning. Needless to say, a fly can't buzz too close to my ear without me getting too excited. This is an example of how my inexperience caused me to make a bad choice. I've learned from that past experience. This is the creation of hindsight. I have a very vivid memory (from the past) that plays a role in how I respect beehives (today) from that one encounter alone. The point is we all have had different experiences in life, and that all were learning opportunities. But how many of us have learned our lessons?

Most of us haven't applied the beautiful privilege of hindsight, so we end up missing life lessons. It's a double-edged sword; on the one hand this failure causes us to repeatedly make the same mistakes. The old saying goes, "you fool me once shame on you fool me twice shame on me". The same rules applied to this too, you make the poor choice the first time then it is only a mistake, you continue to repeat the behavior then its bad decisions. On the other hand, when we have been through something a little more traumatic, it can be difficult to reflect, in fact, it's common to block the memory all together. What happens then is we'll develop triggers to an event that we've tried to forget. That leaves us with a very complicated situation. You have this highly emotional and/or physical response to someone or something that has triggered your memory from a previous trauma. However, that trauma was never addressed. Even if we don't block the memory itself, we can find ourselves feeling wronged and victimized. we can then end up using it as a crutch and justify the need to cope or to act out.

When we leave these issues unresolved, we ultimately carry them with us into the next relationships, whether it be professional or personal. Our past has and will play a role in the way we approach life.

Have you ever put together a jigsaw puzzle? I'm sure you're like "duh?" Well, how did you approach the task the very first time you did it? Did you figure it out on your own? Did someone show you the "easiest" way? Or did you start at the edges like I do? Some of us approach this project in different ways, and that's okay. After all, the goal is to get the puzzle done, correct? Who cares how long it takes? Or what the techniques are as long as we get it done. When you think of perception or perspective, it's like putting a puzzle together. Except the puzzle would be equal to an experience that can have many pieces over a short or long time.

The event that is tantamount to the puzzle is the first time we're faced with a situation in which the moment our perspective is formed. (the picture on the puzzle) Our technique in the way we put it together is dependent on how we experience the moment. That is when our perspective was formed. Whether we start at the edges, or whether we identify colors, it will depend on how we think and/or how we were taught. Humans are creatures of habit, and first impressions are everything! Therefore, we typically approach circumstance the same way that we learned to initially. Sometimes, we learn that there are better ways. Then again, some of us never learn. At the end of the day, we've all been through different situations in life. Some are good, and others are not so good. Nonetheless, they have all affected how we see or perceive, and the way in which we navigate our lives.

Merriam-Webster.com gave a brief but concise definition of the concept and phrase "Tipping Point".

A 'Tipping Point': The critical point in a situation, process, or system beyond which a significant and often unstoppable effect or change takes place.

Think about this definition in mind. When we get to the 'Tipping Point,' and are fed up with the results, we find ourselves ready to make change. For some of us that tipping point looks like a trip to the County Jail. For others, it's waking up in a detoxification center for the umpteenth time. Maybe it's following the same type of guy, and ending up on the bad end of the stick. For some reason rock bottom looks different to all of us. However, when we reach that point and make the decision to change, we have to take a long, hard look at the way we have learned to put together this puzzle of life. We must pause and seriously reflect on the things that we have been through. Particularly, we must reflect on the most uncomfortable moments and not just sit there. We must pay very close attention to how you were before, during and at the conclusion of that event. That is the essence of hindsight. It is being able to reflect on a moment from one past event. It is being able to comprehend now, and it is able to see what we could not understand then.

Foresight

Let's take a look at the definition for the word foresight: Foresight is defined by Webster as:

Foresight -1) The act or power of foreseeing the act of looking forward

2) Beforehand, foresight is also defined as concern for the future

This is the moment we experience something mentally, emotionally or physically. When it causes a response, it becomes a memory that can last a lifetime. The funny thing about people is that we can recall a memory and experience the same feelings that we had when we were actually in the moment. It feels like we can literally smell, taste and feel as if it was happening all over again. Not just that, but we can walk into a restaurant and the aroma of the food or the atmosphere, or perhaps a song can trigger a memory. Have you ever heard old songs that your parents used to play for you and suddenly you are brought back in time to a particular moment? The mind is that incredible and our being is that magnificent. The same way we can have a response to a song, and it triggers a positive memory we can also be triggered by a negative memory. Something as simple as driving through the old neighborhood that we use to get high in can ignite a flood of thoughts.

The privilege of foresight is the understanding of the past, and being able to use that reference point to predict a potential outcome for the future. I remember being a kid when I learned one of the biggest lessons of my life. I sat on the bed in my mother's room while she was teaching my big sister how to iron. She set the iron on the ironing board, plugged it in and waited until it was hot. She was talking to my sister, but by this time, I'm off the bed and in the middle of the two of them. She tells my sister to go get something from the other room. When she gets back, she looks at me calling me by my nickname. She said "Bubba, this iron is very hot! If you touch it, it's going to burn you. So, don't touch it." What I heard was "Bubba, as soon as I look away, touch the iron" I said, "Yes, Mama, and I sat there watching them iron. About five minutes later, I had somehow decided to reach up and try to learn to iron. I touched something that was scorching hot. I don't know if it was the iron or the clothes. What I do know is I was in pain! I saw light flashing in my eyes! It was so hot! Needless to say, I learned that lesson the hard way.

I'm sure that we can all relate in one way or another to this, right? Well, let's reflect on this and see what we can understand about how that one lesson has affected my life. Before our first interaction with something hot, we don't have a true understanding of what "hot" really is. It is fair to say that we have been warned. However, to know what hot is, we had to experience it. so that our sense of touch to gather information or to feel it. However, the second we feel it, we gain a very real perspective. It is a clear picture of what hot really means. For me, from that point forward, or the moment I saw, heard, or even thought about the iron, I remembered the day I was burned by it. Here we are, with an experience we all can relate to. As a result of pain, the sensation of "hot" is ingrained in our memory. It is in such a way that the idea of an iron, stove, lamp, candle, or any other heat source gives the understanding of potential harm. That is a moment from our past, (hindsight) thus creating the power or the ability to foresee the potential outcome of a future event (foresight). Once first-hand account of cause and effect is gained, we become able to foresee future cause and effect to a degree.

For example, have you seen a person standing near a stove with the eye on high? More than likely, knowing if they reach out and touch it, they will scream in pain. They will touch the eye, scream, then turn around, and touch it again. What would you think of this person? What if this person did this weekly, monthly and yearly? Give me five words that you would use to describe this persons' actions.

1) _____

2) _____

3) _____

4) _____

5) _____

Now, let's say that this person is you, and the stove represents an abusive relationship, substance abuse, anger issues, abandonment issues or any other life traps you are struggling with. How do you view that individual now? The aim is to depict a person dealing with a realistic destructive pattern of behavior. Seeing that we have all been through some form of life trap, we must understand that we may experience them in different ways. We all have moments in our past that we can look back on and learn from. The goal is to learn from the mistakes, as well as to be aware of how that moment has helped to form our perspective. Hindsight is the understanding of where certain habits are formed, and where the perspective was developed. Foresight is the ability to refer to the patterns of our past in order to foresee the likely outcome in the future.

Insight

Listed below are two definitions from the Merriam Webster internet dictionary.

Insight-1 the power or act of seeing into a situation: penetration. 2. The act or result of apprehending the inner nature of things or of seeing intuitively.

Perceive-1 become aware or conscious of (something): come to realize or understand.

Insight grants us the ability to be in the moment and gives us a true understanding of the situation. This is the essence of knowledge, and is awareness gained through experience. Let me reiterate hindsight again. It's an understanding of an event that we didn't comprehend at the time. Foresight, however, is the act of foreseeing the future based on our prior experiences. Insight is the ability to comprehend the moment while we are still experiencing it. Insight is also something that we should all strive to obtain. It doesn't make sense for us to continue to learn the same lesson time and time again! We have to approach life from a different angle and learn how to see every moment as an opportunity to learn. We need to add knowledge and wisdom to the man or the woman we are supposed to be. I know that for me personally, that the more I learn about life, the more I realized how much I don't know about life! Then, I began to assess the people around me who have already been through things that I'm going through. I realized that they have already learned these lessons. That motivates me to know more, to read more, to continue to grow, and to mature into the man that I know I can be. This, I'm destined to be. Most importantly, I ask questions. Again, this is just me. However, I've learned mostly all my lessons the hard way, and I'm tired of it! I have finally figured out the power in learning from the experience, instead of forever being the man who only learns from his own experiences.

Everyone is not going to *choose* to grow themselves. Believe me, I'm not trying to sound like you, and I am no better than or less than the next person. I'm just being as transparent as possible. If it was easy to achieve that, then the whole world would be a better place to live. Not to mention the fact that we all know someone who we look at and think to ourselves "This fool just doesn't get it!"

Let me ask you a question. "Have you ever missed an opportunity? I mean flat out missed it?" I know for a fact that I have. Not once but a few times. The way to measure if a person has learned from their past is to watch how they handle the present. When they are faced with the exact circumstances, or a similar set of events and circumstances. If you make the same decision or one just as bad, clearly you have NOT figured it out. We have to ask ourselves, "Why am I missing the mark?" If you legitimately don't understand your behavior or choices then the reflection has to go further back into your past, including those root behaviors that we've spoken about.

However, if you know the "Whys" to your behavior, and are just making silly excuses and decisions. Or perhaps you lack the strength and are stuck in the trap of routine. The question you must ask yourself is, "What has me tethered to bad decisions?" You know better, yet you won't do better. Even the Bible teaches that once you know right from wrong, you are now held doubly accountable. So, what is it?

I once heard someone say the opportunity of a lifetime must be seized within the lifetime of the opportunity. When you dissect those words, you suddenly realize every opportunity has a life-expectancy encoded within it. And it's imperative that you not only see the opportunity as your moment to act. You also realize it has a window of time within it that will yield to you its benefits as well as prosperity. Now, that's pretty prolific isn't it? Did you realize that every opportunity has a lifetime of expectancy? Since you don't know how long of a life this opportunity carries within its potentiality, then you must learn to seize it. Or you may miss the opportunity, experience, and any benefits it carried?

At the end of the day, change is uncomfortable. Whether we're sitting in the trauma of our past, or we're trying to develop new healthy and proactive habits. However, it's in our most uncomfortable moments that real growth occurs. Take a look around yourself this very minute. What do you see? No, not the Cheetos that have been sitting in the middle of living room floor all day, in which everyone who walks by them acts like they are not there. I'm not talking your significant other who's been probably lying next to you snoring while you're reading this book. I mean take a real deep look at the life you built for yourself. Is it what you wanted? I say the "life you've built," because I want to stress the power that we have over our lives. Yes, we all understand that in this life a lot of things will happen that we don't have control over. At the very same time, we do have control over how we respond. Therefore, you are very much responsible for your life. Now, as you take inventory of your current set of circumstances, I want you to take out a piece of paper or open your notepad, and begin to write down all the things that you wish you could change. This is simply to reflect and utilize the privilege of hindsight. In this exercise, I want you to connect the dots between the things you don't like about the present and want to change. Now, ask yourself, "Where do these issues originate in my past?"

The negative experiences of your past are having a negative effect on your approach in the present. That's revealed in hindsight. In the present, you understand that connection and you are becoming aware of your power in creating your present. Being able to see the cause and effect in your past, and being able to see the pattern of behavior that developed allows you to experience it. In the present, this allows you to have a pretty fair prediction of what your future is going to look like if nothing changes. If you own the responsibility of the moment, then your tomorrow will look exactly like you intended it to look. Hindsight, insight, and foresight are the comprehension of our past, the awareness of the present, and the diligence in pursuing the future we envision. Everything that you have ever been through has created the person that you are right now, this very second. You must become aware then it is your responsibility to take control of your life, and you must begin to coach your own growth. This will allow you to move towards the future that you were destined to live.

Self-Image

Self-image, not to be misconstrued with who we are, but instead, is how we see ourselves. The goal is to change, to grow, and to develop into the men and women that we know we can be. However, in order to know what that person looks like we have to start to define who you are now and compare that to what the Ideal you will look like. Here's an exercise. Grab a sheet of paper, and fold it down the middle. On one side, right at the top of the page write "Self –image" and on the other side write "Projected self-image." Now, under self-image write down how you see yourself and be honest. How would you describe yourself physically, emotionally, spiritually, and mentally? In order for this exercise to work, we have to be willing to completely be honest with ourselves. It's the only way to gain insight into who we really are. So, when writing down the self- image description, we must be open about addictions, confidence and negative character traits. The same goes for the projected or the ideal self- image. We have to be open and detailed with who we want to be. We have to be willing to say, "I want them washboard abs that I see in the infomercials!"

Seriously, now is the time to lay out and clearly paint the picture of who we want to be. Yes, be realistic. However, we have to have an in-depth goal to move forward. Once we have our two lists (this may take a few sheets depending on how descriptive you are), began to point out the three most important changes that need to be made from the "Self-image" side and connect them to the "Ideal Self –Image" description. Now, we should have our three most important changes connected to the desired traits.

The next step is to put together a detailed plan on how to go from point A to point B. From insecure to confident, from failure to successful, from dead beat dad to father of the year! At the top of the plan, I want you to write this reminder to yourself, "Nothing is Impossible, because I'm possible" This moment that we're in right here right now is our moment, and nothing can prevent us from moving into the next stage of maturity ... except us.

Self-Image Worksheet

The Goal plan

"Nothing is Impossible because I'm possible"

_____

_____

_____

_____

_____

_____

_____

_____

_____

_____

_____

_____

_____

_____

_____

_____

_____

_____

_____

_____

_____

_____

_____

This is how we should approach any and every goal concerning self-growth. We have to ask ourselves these questions, and break them down into a checklist of sorts. Using this method simplifies what may seem like an unattainable goal. It turns into a handful of smaller goals that are easily attained all the while still moving us toward a desired result. I don 't care what a person 's belief system is. I am not here to challenge, compare or attempt to convert. However, I will share with you that I believe every person has been created for a purpose.

A lot of religions believe that God has a plan for us. While other ideologies suggest that we have full control over the direction in our lives. Your beliefs are respectfully yours. At the core of humanity, both science and religion have been focused on answering two questions. "What created us, and for what purpose?" Again, my goal isn't to challenge your belief system. However, I do want to concentrate less on the "Who" and more on the idea of purpose and the keys to fulfilling it.

Chapter 3

Purpose

"I don't believe you should have the luxury of being bored"

William S. Graham

Purpose is defined as:

Purpose- *The reason for which something is done or something exists.*

The same way we can look back at events throughout our life and then understand the roles that they have played in the direction our lives. These roles have taken us thus far, and we have to understand that the steps we take today direct the path of a future. Because our history serves as a reference point. The failures and successes of others are also templates for us to learn from.

Let's take a look at history, and apply that same way of thinking. Instead of hindsight coming from our own experiences, we can learn life's lessons first-hand. Let's take a look at Elon Musk and Steve Jobs. The goal now elevates one from learning from our own experiences to learning from the experienced person.

As they old saying goes, "There are two ways to learn. One is by trial and error, and the other is by choosing a mentor...always choose a mentor.

Elon Musk

The South African born entrepreneur is most known for founding Tesla Motors, SpaceX, and SolarCity. The son of a Canadian model and a South African engineer, Elon Musk is said to have been so lost in his daydreams about inventions that his parents and doctors ordered a test to see and check his hearing. At age 10, he became interested in computers. He taught himself how to program, and by the age of 12 he sold his first software. It was a game he created called Blastar. By the age of 17, the young Elon Musk moved to Canada from his home in Pretoria, South Africa. He attended Queens University in order to avoid mandatory service in the South African military.

In 1992, he left Canada to study business and physics at the University of Pennsylvania. He graduated with an undergraduate degree in economics, and he stayed for a second degree where he acquired a Bachelor in Physics. After leaving Pennsylvania, Musk headed to Stanford University in California to pursue a PhD in energy physics. However, the Internet boom was erupting at the time. So, he dropped out after two days to become a part of it. He ultimately made his first billion in October 2002 when PayPal was acquired by eBay for 1.5 billion in stock.

Elon Musk went on to start Space X and Tesla Motors. He also purchased SolarCity, which is a Company he helped his cousin start in 2006. In 2017, Musk launched The Boring Company, a Company devoted to boring and building tunnels in order to reduce street traffic. He achieved this and so much more at the ripe age of 48.

When we look at Elon Musk and just a fraction of his accomplishments, we see a person who had a strong interest in inventing as a child. This is so much that he daydreamed about them that caused concerns about his hearing. I mean that's saying a lot in and of itself. Can you remember being a kid and daydreaming about being a movie star, football Player or singer? Ask yourself, "What happened to those dreams?"

A lot of people grow up and come to an understanding that life is real, and those childish dreams are just fantasies. In the real world there are bills that need to be paid, and their kids need to eat. Their purpose becomes limited to the needs of the present. That's the biggest difference between adults and children. Adults know that some things just aren't possible, while kids believe that anything is possible. That shift in perspective is one of the main reasons people give up on pursuing their dreams. For a lot us, those dreams don't seem real anymore. What would happen if we continued to follow our dreams?

Elon Musk also displayed something that was extraordinary when he was just ten years old. He became interested in computers, and he ended up teaching himself how to program and create his own software. That's an amazing accomplishment of a very early age to create and sell your own game at the age of twelve. I know that when I was a kid, I sold candy and shoveled snow. Or I raked leaves trying to earn a couple of dollars. I mean I tried everything short of the lemonade stand. Let me ask you this. Can you think back and remember anything that you were good at? Like playing instruments, sports, or perhaps a spelling bee? Where do you think your life would be if you would have stayed at it? Or had an opportunity to develop those skills?

Some of us were dreamers, fantasizing about doing certain things and there wasn't anything that could come in and change that dream. While others had talents, some developed others not so refined. Still somehow, they became faded dreams or they just passed away through the process of time.

Imagine your day to day life being able to wake up and make more than just a living. How about instead of playing video games for fun or singing in the shower, envision yourself designing games or singing on the grand stage in front of thousands. Well the truth is that nothing is impossible. History has shown us that. So, when you pick up the paint brush and began to convey the art of your mind on the canvas, remember that the only difference between your art and art on the walls in the top galleries could be something simple as tenacity, courage and forbearance.

The key to fulfilling purpose is to do what you are passionate about doing. Choose the career of your passion. This is opposed to working and spending your time and energy supporting the passions of your employer's. Your focus has to be on self. And the moment we shift our perspective to see our worth and to understand that anything is possible; we will begin to live in our purpose. If you are a parent, and have feelings that it may be too late, please don't believe that. It's only too late when you leave this earth. It's never too late to be who you are created to be. Sometimes it's as simple as taking a step towards your dream and watching doors of opportunity began to open for you.

Without being taught, there are people who just innately follow their dreams and the young Elon Musk is one of them. He had dreams, and he had the audacity to follow them. He went to college, where he studied business and physics. He gained degrees and then sensing his moments he dropped out of school two days in. Mind you, to take part in the internet boom at the 90s. Who drops out of Stanford takes part in an unproven industry? Yet he believed in his dreams. These are the same dreams that he had as a child, and they became the very fuel to drive his cars and as of today, they launch his rockets out of this earth. Fulfilling them became his purpose in this life. From where I'm sitting, he seems to be doing pretty well. Not just for himself, but also for the advancement of modern technology.

When we look back at our own experiences, we learned by reflecting on how we felt, how we experienced the event, and how it changed us. However, when we take a look at someone else's story, their failures, and successes, we have to understand what we're looking for. It's not just the inspiration of those successes or the sadness of their tragedy. It's about the lessons that they have learned and that are displayed in their story. It's the formula of hindsight, foresight, and insight. When we began to breakdown the cause and effect of their healthy habits as well as their unhealthy or unproductive ones, we will begin to see a pattern.

In school, I hated history. However, as I'm able to look back and see the importance of it, I'm more a fan than I ever could have imagined. Think about it. Not only do I have my own past experiences to draw lessons from, but I also have all of recorded history. Look at the habits of the worlds' greatest and they'll show you a pattern of great behavior in perspective. I can't tell you what made Elon Musk tick, however I can take a look at the man's life and point out a few things. I can you tell that he was a great dreamer and he followed those dreams. He gained from an education that was in direct support of the career field that he was so passionate about. He was a risk taker as well. You only have one life to live. If you are not living a life of purpose, then what's the point? We all have had dreams and visions at one point or another. However, only a few of us have followed them let alone, have had some success. We have had the ability to look back over our lives and reflect as well as study the great men and women that have come before us. The next time you read of self-help book, try to look deeper into the message. Pay attention to the references and who is telling the story. I'm sure that the author is pulling from their own personal experience as well as the observation of someone else's experiences and/or some historical reference. It is research plus unique perspective. As well as articulation, it creates a well put together self -help book. That, in and of itself, is the essence of how people have learned to learn from one another. That being said, let's see what we can learn from Steve Jobs.

Steve Jobs

"Working hard for something we don't care about
is called stress; working hard for something we love
is called passion"

- Anonymous

Born February 24, 1955 in San Francisco, CA. Steve Jobs was adopted by Paul and Clara Jobs. In 1961, the family moved to Mountain View California just south of Palo Alto which was becoming a center for electronics from the basic elements of devices such as radios, television, stereos and computers. At that time, people started to refer to that area as of the Silicon Valley. As a child, Steve swam competitively but he wasn't really interested in team sports or other group activities. He showed an early interest in electronics and gadgetry. He spent a lot of time working in a garage workshop of a neighbor who worked at Hewlett-Packard an electronic manufacturer. He also saw engineers demonstrate new products. He saw his first computer at the age of 12. He knew right away that he wanted to work with computers. In high school, Jobs attended lectures at the Hewlett-Packard plant. On one occasion, he boldly asked William Hewlett, the President of the Company, for some parts he needed to complete for a class project. Hewlett was so impressed that he gave Jobs the parts and offered him a summer internship at Hewlett-Packard.

Jobs graduated high school in 1972 and went on to Reed College in Portland, Oregon for two years. He dropped out after one semester to visit and study eastern religions in the summer of

1974. In 1975 he joined a group called the Hebrew Computer Club where he met Steve Wozniak. In 1976 they formed their own computer company. Thus, the Apple company was born.

Jobs and Wozniak had opened an entirely new market ushering in the personal computer era. Jobs was the marketing force behind Apple. In early 1983, he unveiled the Lisa. It was designed for people with minimal computer experience. However, it didn't sell well because it was more expensive than some of the personal computers sold by its competitors at that time. IBM was Apple's biggest competitor. In 1984, Apple introduced a revolutionary new model, the Macintosh, which was very easy to use. However, it didn't sell well either to businesses because it lacked a few favorable features such as corresponding high-quality printer. That failure was the beginning of Jobs' downfall at Apple. In 1995, he resigned from the very company that he had founded, although he kept his position as chairman of its board of directors. Job soon hired some of his former employees to begin a new computer company called "Next," and late in 1998, the "Next" computer was introduced. It was aimed at the education department. While the initial reactions were good (the product was user friendly, had fast processing speed, excellent graphics display with an outstanding sound system.) However, the "Next" machine never caught on. It was too costly, had a black and white screen and wasn't able to be linked to other computers. It also lacked the ability to run common software.

Yet another failure, however, it still wasn't the end of Jobs. In 1986, Jobs purchased the computer graphics division called Pixar from filmmaker George Lucas. This same computer-animated film production released Toy Story. Nine years later, the huge box office hit Pixar went on to make Toy Story Il and A Bug's Life, which Disney distributed in Monsters Inc. It had the largest opening weekend ticket sales of any animated film in history. In December of 1996, Apple purchased NeXT software costing $400 million dollars. Jobs returned to Apple as a part time consultant as the CEO. Over the next six years, Apple introduced several new products and marketing strategies. In 1997, Jobs announced Apple with sell computers directly to users over the Internet and by telephone. The Apple store became a runaway success. Within a week it was the third largest E-commerce site on the Internet. That year Jobs was named interim CEO of Apple. In February of 1996, a Times Magazine article quoted Jobs saying, "The thing that drives me and my colleagues is that you see something very compelling to you and you don't quite know how to get it, but you know sometimes intuitively it's within your grasp and it is worth putting in years of your life to make it come into existence."

Steve Jobs is one of the most influential people in modern history. Looking at his life, what patterns of behavior stand out to you? At a very young age, he shows a strong interest in electronics. He worked around them, joined a club with electronics manufacturing company, Hewlett-Packard, where he eventually attended lectures. Jobs even approached the president of the company and made such an impression that he earned an internship there. He was in pursuit of his passion from the very start. He even tried his hand at swimming. However, he wasn't interested. His heart was in gadgetry. Every step of the way he pursued his interest, and he became a successful businessman in an industry that he helped pioneer. Like anyone, he faced adversity, and yet that was not enough to deny him what was his. He continued to follow his dreams and passions, and sometimes those risks don't pay off. Yet, he still chose to chase his dreams. When he had to resign from his own company, he could have retired and enjoyed the fortune he had earned. Did he? Absolutely not! He continued to move forward like a person driven by purpose. I don't know if he had known that he would be one of the men to change the way the world would use computers, but in staying true to himself and never giving up on what he believed in, he would ultimately chart a course that only he would be able to navigate. Imagine Steve Jobs quitting after being faced with such failure. What would the world look like today?

What if he didn't take that one risk? What would your cell phone look like? What functions would it have? What would we use to transfer money online, if not for Elon Musk? How would that look? Now, along those same lines, imagine yourself living a life of purpose. What would your life look like if you had not quit the football team? Or if you would have stayed in college? Or if you would have taken that one job? Listen, I understand more than you know. The bills have to be paid, and the baby has to eat. I get it. At the very same time, how much longer are you going to stay in the same cycle that you have been in? How much longer are you going to continue working 40 hours plus a week to further someone else's dreams? I'm not saying it's easy, but what I am saying is that it's not impossible! I'm also so very much aware that the moment we have children something changes within us. The light comes on, and we suddenly realize that it's not just me now. It's us, and we began to live life a little bit differently. We are now living to provide food, water, shelter, and security to our children. Nothing else in the world seems to matter. This is true, but we also must be aware of this, our responsibilities as parents extend far beyond providing these basic needs. We also have to support healthy cognitive growth and development. We have to ensure that the next generation is afforded the opportunity that we failed to capitalize on. They have to be able to have an understanding that anything is possible if they would only believe, and have the audacity to follow those dreams. The lessons displayed in the lives of Steve Jobs and Elon Musk, as well as the lessons of our own lives are opportunities to exercise hindsight. Study the lives of the greats that have come before you, and, reflect on the tough lessons that life has taught you. Learn to recognize the cause and effect of your actions and inactions. Take that understanding and apply it in a forward-thinking perspective learning to use vision. You can foresee the results you can have if you put in the work as well as the headaches you'll avoid having when you have been there and done that. Develop insight and understand the beauty in this very moment. Know that if you believe it, then you can achieve it. Nothing is *impossible* because *I'm possible*! However, to have what you have never had, you must learn to do what you have never done. Change is truly inevitable! Once you understand that your change *will* happen, maybe you can take back the power in your own life. I promise you this. You can either change your life, or you can sit back and then let life change you. The definition of purposes is "an intended or desired result." What's your purpose? Take a look at your day-to-day life, and ask yourself how many hours have you dedicated to pursuing purpose? Then compare that same time and energy to what you spend working on someone else's. If you are not happy with that comparison, then something has to change.

Not only have that but parents and leaders/mentors throughout the community bared a larger responsibility than the rest of the world. You have to invest into the children, and that helps you sleep in Formula One in purpose really looks like. You have to pay attention to their strong suits and interests. Talk to them, and learn and encourage the growth in their passions. Learn to cultivate their talents. After all, LeBron James would not be the best basketball player of the planet without someone investing in his growth maturity. However, the next generation is looking to you, and to us for this support. We can't fail them! We just can't.

"Every positive change in life begins with a clear unequivocal decision that you're going to either do something or stop doing something"

-Anonymous

Chapter 4

Dreams and Vision…Yours vs. Theirs

*"The best way to predict the future is to create it" -
Peter Drucker*

Dreams are defined as:

Dream- *1) a series of mental images, thoughts, and
emotions occurring in certain stages of sleep.*

2) Hopes or aspirations.

By now we have had time to think back and reflect on life
in a totally different light. We have been down memory lane a few
times, had a couple of emotional moments, and dared to revisit the
uncomfortable feelings of trauma and the role that it has played in
creating the men and women that we are today. We have even had
the chance to discuss "dreams" to an extent. Now, I want to take a
closer look at dreams in a different way and the influences that can
mold or shape our lives and those around us. Right now, I want
you to take a few seconds to think about your last dream, literally.
What were you doing? Who was there, and what did you feel? Can
you think about any reoccurring dreams or maybe one that you
have had as a child? As we dive into dreams, pay close attention to
yours, and where they may come from.

Change…The Inevitable
Christopher J. Taylor

The funny thing about a dream is it's not real! Dreaming has been something that has raised questions in humanity since the beginning of time. Even in the Bible, in Ecclesiastes 5:3b. "For a dream cometh through the multitude of business…". Some people believe that dreams have some type of futuristic warning or prophetic meanings and hold them in very high in esteem. While others will tell you it's simply the brain activity while the body is in a resting mode or sleeps. Nonetheless, we all can agree that dreams can feel real as though it really happened, right? I mean, just ask anybody no matter what age they are. Even in adulthood, we have these dreams that we're able to see, hear, smell, and touch as though they were actually experienced. If you have ever been through a traumatic event, suffer from PTSD (Post Traumatic Stress Disorder), or recently suffered a loss of a family or loved one, then you know how real dreams can be. It's important to bring this into the conversation, because, the very thing that makes some dreams "feel" real are the fact that our senses respond the same way during subconscious dreams as they do in real life. That's a testament to the power and capability of the human mind. Because we can "experience" a dream, then our dreams can play a role in our perception. However, the second we open our eyes, we no longer have access to that realm, and we suddenly find ourselves back in this time and place.

Our dreams, hopes, and aspirations are exactly the same. We can have all of the talent, athletic abilities, and/or intelligence in the world. As long as they stay in the "dream world" they will only amount to a "series of mental images, thoughts and emotions". It's not until you dream of something in the future, that the dream becomes a vision. It's interesting to use this word vision, because our eyes are the senses of the flesh used to give us sight i.e., vision. But we also realize that vision is not limited to physical attributes.

Vision is defined:

Vision- *the faculty of sight, the unusual ability and for seeing what is going to happen.*

Right now, I want you to understand that this is your moment. Once you become aware, it is your responsibility to take control of the direction of your life. We have used the words "dreams" throughout the first half of this book for the reason of common understanding. However, from here on out, we will use the word vision for the purpose of insight! Dreams are not real regardless of how real they feel. *You* are what turn ideas into reality. The second you set a goal and begin to walk towards it becomes vision! The moment you can see or foresee what the healthier you look like, and began to take action; you are now walking in vision. We have to learn to move with specific intent, and to live with purpose. As you sit back and began to access your life, just think about whose dreams you have been dreaming. Are you being true to yourself? When you think about what you want in life is it really what *you* want? Or, is it what people expect of you? Has society created a societal norm and are we unconsciously attempting to try to fit in it? I mean really think about it and be honest. I know that in certain communities wearing name brand clothes and expensive shoes are a sign of status. While in some of the other communities these things have zero importance. Depending on where a person is raised and/or what that persons' examples are will dictate the way their perspectives are formed. So, becoming aware of all these particular influences, we have to again step back and see what has created the perspective and determine if these are really my likes and dislikes? Is it an outside influence shaping the way that I see things? Whose dreams have you really been dreaming?

Along those same lines, whose purpose have you been fulfilling? Don't shake your head now because if we were going to be honest with self, you and I both know that you can say what you want but your actions speak your truth and if we look at your actions or inactions what are they going to say? Looking at your actions and not your words is the true measure of a person.

Take a second to bring the next generation into the conversation. Be it your children or kids around the neighborhood or any young people who may be looking at you as an example. How do you think you are influencing that person? Are you a good example? How are you affecting their perspective? Have you been living vicariously through them?

Throughout this brief time, we've had together, we've gone over how the things we experience as children can have a lasting imprint on how we see and approach life. That being said, we have been able to understand that we are now in the same position of our parents when they were kids. The difference between today and yesterday is that we are aware of the power that we possess, which is the power of responsibility! We are not just responsible for ourselves. but for any and every one that looks to us for an example of success. This is for anyone who is looking for leadership, mentorship, and our guidance in how to navigate their journey called life. Because we have life experience, it's our responsibility to turn and invest in the next generation. Otherwise we would be failing them. We must not drop the ball the way so many members of our community did in the past. We've learned this lesson already first-hand, and we have survived its aftermath. Now we must do everything within our power to provide a template of success.

That means we have to learn to lead by example as well as support the cognitive maturity of the youth. We can't live vicariously through them. To do that would do nothing but rob them of their individuality and of their purpose.

When we talk about the youth, we have to remember that they're watching everything we do from the way we'd walk and talk to the way we treat our significant others. They will pick up on our sarcasm, accents and mannerisms. It's in these first twenty years of life that a lot of first experiences happened. That being said, this is the most important developmental stage and we have to be aware of that. The goal is to allow them to have their own dreams and to support those ambitions as well as teach them the steps to turning dreams into visions.

Not only have that, but parents and leaders/mentors throughout the community bared a larger responsibility than the rest of the world. You have to pay attention to their strong suits and interests. Talk to them, learn and encourage their growth and pursuit of passions. Learn to cultivate their talents. After all, LeBron James would not be the best basketball player of the planet without someone investing in his growth development. We can't fail them! We just can't.

As we begin to take on this new approach to the way that we lead, we have to be disciplined with the way that we encourage that means that when our sons show strong aptitude in theater and we think that he should be playing sports. We must remember that it's not about the life we want him to live, but it's about supporting his or her ambitions and strong suits. This isn't going to be easier said than done. Of course, every parent wants the best for their kids, and every mentor feels that their job is to direct the one being mentored. That's to be expected. However, the second we begin to push in the direction we want them to go in, that's the second we begin to impose on their dreams. Whether they express it or not, when we fail to support their individuality, we contradict the idea that they can be anything that they want to be. That is the beginning of "inside the box" thinking.

"Do something uncomfortable today by stepping out of your box. You don't have to settle for what you are- you get to create who you want to become"

Howard Walstein

The "box" is the realm of possibility. What's in the box is possible, but what's outside the box is impossible. Children are born without thinking constraints. We live in a day and a society where you don't need to use your imagination. The television industry will stagger the imagination from infancy. We live in a world of commercialism bombarding you constantly subliminally and consciously 24/7. The right to choose has been taken from you, and the power to think has been suppressed to almost nothing. You can live in a world of imagination where people can fly through the sky, and dragons can roam through the earth thousands of years ago. In a world where the fruit can talk and the boogie man is your neighbor. You can still believe that anything is possible, and anything will be possible.

Have you ever thought about how powerful the human mind is? The young mind hasn't learned that in this world we have universal laws and some things we just can't do. It's learning lessons like touching the hot iron for the first time or feeling the excruciating pain of being stung by a bee that your perspectives are formed. It's the parents telling the child that their dreams of being a singer are stupid and impossible that each walls of the "box" is constructed.

The first twenty years of life are spent collecting data of gaining life experiences, and that is what will dictate who we will become. A lot of people think inside that box because it's the only way they know how to think. Others fall into the habit of making excuses and justifications which end up creating the self-imposed limitations. It's just one of those causes and effects, or things that we've talked about before. We have to look at how we were raised in order to understand where we have created some of these life traps within our own lives. With that, we have to own the way we speak, demonstrate, and influence those around us which can create their life traps as well.

The good thing about change is that it's inevitable! The second we change the way we see life... the life we see will begin to change. Sometime it's as small as removing the word can't from your vocabulary. That alone will have life altering effects. Think about your perspective. Are you one of those people who are always saying that things can't be done because of this or that, and it will never work? Well, this is an exercise especially for you.

Find yourself a space that is closed in preferably a corner of a room. Or if you are an outdoor sort of person, go to the backyard and walk to the corner of the fence. Stand approximately three feet away from the corner. The fence will represent what's impossible or what can't be done, the corner of the box. Now think of a goal that you have had in the last year. As you began to step towards the goal (go ahead and take a step physically towards the fence) There, you'll notice that you can go far because there's a wall of impossibility that stands between where you are and where you need to go. So, toss that goal aside. Let's think of another goal and try to step towards it. Did you hit another dead end? Dead ends will sound something like this, "That will never work" or "They only give those types of people loans". As long as we have this inside the box, kind of closed-minded thinking, will always be our Story; we will never reach our greatest self because we have these self-imposed limitations. As you stand in this corner, I want you to simply turn around. With the open space to your front and the corner to your back, turn around your thinking and put your face to the open realm of possibility. Now walk towards those goals and tell me what happens next? The opposite of I can't is...I can.

The only thing that can happen at this point is you become successful in obtaining what you set your heart to obtain. It's the change in perspective that opens the door to whatever direction you want to go in. Life is going to throw all kinds of obstacles in your way, but you don't have to throw roadblocks in your own way. We must be the change that we wish to see. That old saying, "Do as I say and not as I do" is failing us. Know the difference between dreams and visions. Encourage growth and development, and show the next generation how to follow their dreams by following yours.

Tell me, what is your vision? What does it look like? What are you doing to help your vision come into fruition? Who shares it, and what is it going to take to get you there?

"When you under value what you do, the world will undervalue who you are".

Oprah Winfrey

Change...The Inevitable
Christopher J. Taylor

You would be surprised at how many people are living this journey called life, but don't have any idea where it's going! They are literally along for the ride. No judgment here. I understand someone has to be the leader, and someone has to be the follower somebody has to be the employer, and somebody has to be the employee. Someone has to be a shepherd, and someone has to be the sheep. We have to remember if it is okay to follow in some situations. Every good leader has to know how when to follow so there is nothing wrong with that. However, we only have one life and it is a short one. I promise you this, with that being said, the personal investment has to start with oneself. We have to be in the driver seat of our lives, and not always the passengers. That would be the equivalent to your life being the movie, and you not being the lead actor. It just doesn't make sense to not assume your rightful position as leader in your own life.

What does this quote mean to you, "When you under value what you do, the world will undervalue who you are?" As long as you play yourself short, the world will continue to short change you! It's as simple as that. The moment you realize who you are, with the value you bring to any room you enter. When you realize the greatness that's within you, everything changes. Your conversations will change, your work habits will intensify, as your true purpose suddenly comes forth. The perspective here is the key! This is the rule that we must learn to operate in as we begin building the next noble generation.

Change

Right this minute, the world is on a complete shutdown due to the Coronavirus pandemic. I mean in the course of a day, life as we knew it came to a halt. As we attempt to slow the spread of the novel virus; the way that we interact with one another and socialize has changed. The emergence of COVID-19 has had and will continue to have a rippling effect on the broader community at large. With a government shutdown, businesses will go under, meaning that people will lose jobs, companies will close, and businesses will be forfeited potentially forever. No matter how much government funded stimulus checks are sent out, it won't be enough to get everyone through this time. The loss of life has been catastrophic! Some families have lost multiple members at the hands of this virus in a matter of days. I mean, this is one of the toughest times humanity has seen in the last one hundred years.

The crazy thing about this is that it seemingly happened overnight! It too can be summed up in one word, which is change. I mean, when we think about it, people have been adapting to our environment since the very beginning right? Well, it would be very naive of us to think that we're the only living organism that evolved. Again, history has been our best teacher. Think about the different outbreaks as recently as today, the Corona Virus aka Covid 19, or a few centuries ago, the Bubonic plague, the Ebola, the Spanish flu, etc., It happened before, it's happening now, and it will happen again. We cannot stop it unless we can learn from the past failures, and glean from the success. Thus, making us better to prepare and curtail or at least control it.

The point is we can grow. Evolution and change is encoded in our DNA. If viruses, plants, and animals, in fact, all living things can adapt and change for the better or worse than surely, we can. Change is a universal law and there is nothing that anyone can do to stop it! We can, however, learn how to control the changes that we are responsible for.

Change…The Inevitable
Christopher J. Taylor

Chapter 5

The Lesson in Being Uncomfortable

"Pain is never wasted"

Francine Segura

By now, we should have a pretty good understanding of how the things we've been through can have an influential role in how we see and approach life. Changing that perspective is one of the keys to real change. When we change our thinking, ultimately our behavior changes as well. We also must become aware that we are in control of change. This is the same way the past plays a role in shaping the present. The present plays a role in shaping our future. That being said, the past can no longer hold us accountable or force us to do anything detrimental. Which means it can no longer stunt our growth. We are in our rightful roles as lead players in this game.

Now the next step is to acquire a working knowledge of how to change. The funny thing about growth is it doesn't have to abide by rules, so to speak. It's something that happens in all sorts of ways, at different times and under different circumstances. Sometimes change is slow and steady. While other times it's instantaneous. One thing is for sure it is going to happen!

Change...The Inevitable
Christopher J. Taylor

Let me share another remarkable time in my life. I remember being a kid, and going outside with my friends to play in the snow. For those of you that didn't know I'm from Denver,

Colorado, the weather here is something quite different! I don't know how the local meteorologists can keep a job trying to predict this weather. Anyways, we're kids and are literally clueless on how to think about anything down the road. So, I go outside and it's cold, but it's not *too* cold. Of course, my father with all his wisdom tells me, "Boy, you better put on a jacket. I tell him "It's not that cold." He then shakes his head and says You're going to learn that fat meat is greasy." See, I don't understand that saying, so I just run off to play with my friends. We start messing around in the snow and throwing snowballs around and the next thing I know it starts to get cold, like *really* cold. Well, I guess you don't need me to finish telling you how the story ended, but in case you do, I almost froze to death that day.

Have you ever found yourself outside, maybe underdressed, and the weather changes completely? I know I have, and on this particular day when I was out playing, I decided to hang out and keep throwing snowballs regardless of how cold I was. It wasn't long before my body took over, and I became very uncomfortable. It had reached its tipping point! I had to call it quits, and I ran home as fast as I could. When I got home my dad was sitting in the living room watching TV. I walked in the door, freezing, frozen, snot hanging from my nose, and my entire body was shaking. He looked at me and didn't say a word. I tried to void eye contact and I walked back towards my room but before I was able to reach the end of the hallway I heard him say "I told you so," and he burst out laughing. Now, I'm going to be honest. It wasn't the last time I went out in the cold without being properly dressed for the weather. However, it wasn't until I was much older that I was able to understand the lesson of "You're going to learn, that fat meat is greasy"

Has anything like that ever happened to you? How did you react? Did you turn and run home? Or were you like me and tried to weather it out and all in the name of play? What kind of reaction did your body have? You see, the human body is without a doubt a phenomenal instrument. Just like the mind, it has both a conscious and subconscious state. The body has voluntary and involuntary functions.

When the body gets cold, the conscious mind will make a decision to find warmth or to tough it out. The body, on the other hand, will automatically respond in the way that it was designed to when we get cold. One of the first signs that the body is cold is when you get goose bumps. This appears to be the body's natural reaction to cold. After being in the cold environment, the skin will attempt to rebalance its surface temperature back to 98.6. According to research, the stimulus of the cold condition causes the tiny muscles attached to each hair follicle to contract. As the temperature continues to drop, the body will continue to react. Once the core body temperature drops, the next response is shivering. That's when the skeletal muscles begin to shake into small movements, creating warmth by expanding energy. I'm not a medical doctor or scientist, but I'm basically repeating what I read and experienced.

First of all, look at the way the body responds to being cold. The survival instinct that is within all us is truly amazing, right? The moment we get cold, the skin gets all goose fleshly, with a warning of sorts as well as an attempt to warm itself back up. When that doesn't work and the body temperature begins to get dangerously low, the muscles begin to shiver. That's the time to really change the situation, because if you stay in that moment without change, the next step is imminent death. Look at the lesson that nature offers us. You can either change your situation, or your situation will change you!

I had an ample opportunity to go and get a coat, or just go home to the warmth of the house. Yet I failed to act. I missed the mark to make a conscious choice. I failed to change my situation, and as a result my body took control of the situation. How many times have you been in a position to change, and failed to do so? I mean, seen all the signs that this is not going to end well? Yet, like a kid on a rollercoaster ride, you just sat there and let life spiral out of control. How many times have you hung out with the wrong crowd? They are the one your Mom and Dad warned you that they were no good, and yet you still hung out with them only to find yourself in between a rock and a hard place? There are lessons and blessings in everything that we go through in this life and I promise you, pain is never wasted. I made the same poor decision, and I went outside without consideration of the weather. However, I learned as I matured and because as a child. I did childish things, but when I became a man, I put away both childish things and did the things as a man should do.

Here is a question for you. Do you do the things that an adult should do? Or are you still making the poor, ill-advised decisions of a child? I'd be a complete fool if I went outside in the snow today to play without a coat. It is said, "Hindsight is the best sight..." I've learned that lesson the hard way. When you look back over your experiences, have you really applied the lessons that were learned?

Change...The Inevitable
Christopher J. Taylor
"Greatness begins beyond your comfort zone"

Robin Sharma

There is a lesson in being uncomfortable. For in this place, you will gain the most growth in so many areas of your life. It is also where we reach our tipping points, and they are the crucible of transformation. Someone noted how change for the better can come when things seem to be at its worst. Like I said earlier, change can happen in numerous ways. We know that if we sit back and live in a place of comfort, it can produce horrible habits of inactivity. Life will take the reins and change us how it sees fit. The lesson has to be that when we take back our power of responsibility, and we diligently pursue the changes that we desire. Therefore, our circumstances will respond accordingly. That will only happen the moment we began to coach growth and move into walking with vision. There is a similar pattern between the human responses of being uncomfortable and the thought process when in a difficult situation. Most people tend to sit in their comfort zone until they reach their own tipping point. The tipping point for you may not be the same as it is for the next person, and it may come in different forms such as traumas of some sort. Other forms may be slow and steady in the buildup. Then one day you look around in total shock wondering, "How did I let this happen?" Like I stated earlier, this human body/mind is an amazing creation! We know that a lot of our instinctual functions are hardwired in a subconscious level of thought. Just think of your fight or flight responses. At the same time, we have been gifted the great power of choice, as well as the opportunity of hindsight foresight, and insight! When things began to get rough, we have the ability to make an informed decision. This is one that is by design intended to better our circumstances.

It's as simple as being cold and making the choice to get a coat. Now that's taking back your power! No more sitting around while life is kicking us in the face, NO! We do not take the reactive stance any longer! From here on, we are the offense. We are forever thinking forward and proactive doers! Life will yield to our plans, and we will now have a voice as well as a strong hand in the direction ones' life is headed. We do not wait to reach the point where things get out of control forcing us into unforeseeable harm. We now know that we can ride the curve of change and face crisis in order to reach a desired result.

Perspective is paramount to the way we utilized experiences from the past as tools for seeing the potential outcomes in our futures. We have to take on a new perspective and learn how to welcome discomfort, while, knowing that it is a sign that growth is the by-product of it. Ask anybody who does any kind of training, from weight lifting to sports, from cycling to dance; the process of training is a very uncomfortable one. It's a lot of early mornings and late nights, as well as bumps and bruises and sore body parts. It's not an easy thing to do at all. It remains as consistent as possible pushing your will to its breaking points day after day.

However, in order for those muscles to develop, repetition is required. It is said that muscles have memory, and this is required to develop stamina, strength, and resilience. In order to become as smooth as silk, it's going to take hard work. Think about the term "growing pains." I assure you it's not called that because it's a pleasant feeling. In fact, it is quite the contrary. I'm thinking it's called that because it hurts! Let's take a look at Steve Harvey's story. We'll see if there is a lesson to be learned from someone who's pretty successful.

Steve Harvey

"Life will only change when you become more committed to your dreams than you are to your comfort zones"

-Anonymous.

"Steve Harvey was once forced to steal gas from gas stations to make ends meet" as reported by Emily Strom and Ann Lindsey Camille. Not the kind of news article caption that you'd expect to see associated with the hardest working man in show business is it? Well, it is true. Steve Harvey has experienced some very hard times early in his life and career including living out of his car and surviving on Bologna sandwiches.

Has anyone ever had to survive off of baloney before? Oh, don't act like I'm the only one, (smile) okay? What about Top Ramen noodles? Perhaps now I'm talking your language. The worst thing about being homelessness is not knowing from day to day, or night after night, where you will sleep. I don't know what's more uncomfortable, not knowing where you are going to lay your head? Or not knowing where you're going to have your next meal. But how does a person change, evolving and going from homeless to being worth 100 million?

In 1985, Steve Harvey won fifty dollars at his first standup comedic contest. After that, he quit his insurance salesman job in pursuit of a career as a standup comedian. Following his passion, needless to say, did not go over well with Marcia, his wife at the time. Considering the fact that he was married and had twins Brandi and Karli naturally, added more pressure than usual. Being the bread winner for them only made taking the chance even more risky. It's one thing to take the risk when its only you. When you factor in a wife and children, the whole dynamics of survival change.

In his first year, Harvey made just three thousand as a comedian. Further down the road he and his wife ended up separating and the relationship he had with his daughters naturally fell apart. With seventy-five percent of his check going to Marcia and the twins, he was forced to live on as little as fifty dollars a week. It's a period that he described as being ugly. "I've made some bad decisions." He even said, "It was crushing. I realized I'm on my own...l have nothing and no one. All I know how to do is make people laugh."

Harvey was forced to steal fuel from gas stations. This was a way to get to comedy gigs which would occasionally put him up in a hotel for a night. Otherwise, his only other choice would be to sleep in his Ford Tempo using an igloo cooler as a makeshift refrigerator. He had to shower at Rest Stop bathrooms and surviving largely on the Bologna sandwiches. Once while attempting to wash up in the sink of a hotel restroom, he was forced to hide in the stall for hours until all the guests left. Steve said I sat down and just started crying but then I heard a voice that said "If you keep going, I'm going to take you places you've never been". It was like God said, "Don't quit, you are almost there."

Not long after that, he finally got his big break in the form of a televised gig at the Apollo. The rewards you get just from persevering and enduring definitely pay off in the long run if you can endure the long run (pun intended). It is obvious that Steve did not quit. He stayed consistent, endured discomfort of the shame and the humiliation. Today, thirty-five years later, we can all say it definitely paid off.

Cool story huh? The thing that blows me away is Steve Harvey is not the only person who had hard times and found a way to turn struggle into success. Look at the list of a few people who were at one time or another homeless, and see if you recognize any of their names. There's Jennifer Lopez known as J-Lo, Michael O'Hare, Jewel, Sylvester Stallone, Halle Berry, Heather Mills, Drew Carey, Jim Cramer, Chris Pratt, and Tyler Perry just to name a few.

These days, the comedian-author, and talk show host who is now married to wife Marjorie, sits comfortably at the helm of an empire estimated to be worth one hundred million. It is a fortune amassed from lucrative standup appearances, bestselling books, movie adaptations, multiple radio, and television gigs. This includes hosting the renowned Family Feud both in the United States and in Africa. He's also hosted and owned the Steve Harvey show and the NBC variety show Little Big Shots.

This is an excellent example of how our worst of days can be the very process of our progress. However, it's in our perspective of this moment that we will determine the fruits of our labor Now, a person can point to different factors in each of these celebrities' lives. However, one thing I'd like to point out, is the common denominator. This is the fact that they have all experienced the struggle and the feelings of being down and out, with nowhere to go. I assume a strong sense of uncertainty naturally rides this beast of burden. Have you ever been there before? Have you ever been run through the ringer? It felt like there was no way out, or that you had lost it all? I have and I'm banking that all of us in some form or fashion have been there before. That again is the common denominator in the lives of the human race.

History has shown us on a worldwide level that people have survived the most uncomfortable and the most incredibly difficult times. Whether it was coming through violent weather storms that have destroyed their homes, families and jobs. Or sickness so terrible that it ultimately ended by the loss of a limb or life of a beloved one. Of course, our experiences differ in many ways, but we all know the adversary of discomfort, which is personally up-close and hands on.

The same is true in our response to discomfort, pain and heartache. Many years ago, I was told, "Crisis rides the curve of change". People think they hate change, but in reality, what they really hate is the crisis that change produces. Many times, crisis doesn't mean you doing something wrong... sometimes it means you're doing everything right. Imagine that is you. It is said so people often know they need to change for one reason or another but because of their fear and hate of the discomfort of change. This is often great or intense. They fight and refuse to ride the curve, and thus, forfeit the outcome. Ultimately, they lose the moment and the process. This cancels the benefits only granted at the end.

We are all unique and handled things differently, but what if I told you that it doesn't have to be that way?

What if I told you that you could choose your responses? Which in turn, puts you in a position to have more fruitful, prosperous outcomes? Does that sound good? Can you see a little better into the forest of life? Let's continue a little further into the next chapter and see if life can bring forth a better future.

Change...The Inevitable
Christopher J. Taylor

Chapter 6

The Power of Choice

*"You eat what you kill meaning your accomplishments are
only the evidence of the work you put in"*

-Rory Atkins

One of the most distinctive characteristics we have is our ability to live the life that we choose by making informed choices. It's our logic, deductive reasoning. Its amazing gift of being able to reflect on an experience in the past, make a decision in the present, with a fair understanding of how it will affect or create our future. The thing about it is, we display this life of choice all the time, yet we live it as if we don't have a choice in the matter at all.

How many times have you heard someone say, "If it isn't broke, don't fix it?" If you've ever owned or driven a car perhaps, and there were times you have seen the check engine light comes on, only to keep driving anyway? These are examples of how we'll overlook or prolong a task or an issue until it's too late. Then, we complain about things as if we are the victim all of a sudden. Imagine this scenario. You're living from paycheck to paycheck, which is an unfortunate financial forecast of many people in our world. Just about all Americans are struggling particularly in light of this global pandemic that has overtaken the world. Imagine that

you're living the best that you can and you really don't have a substantial amount of savings. Then suddenly the car breaks down. Now all of a sudden, it's Ubers, Lyft and Taxi cabs to the rescue. If you are lucky, you can call a friend when you need to get around town or back and forth from home to work. I would say that, all this happened unexpectedly. However, we all know you've seen the check engine light come on at least two weeks ago. What a headache right?

Life in many ways is a lot like the cars we drive. You are on the road and it's a journey. Then the next thing you know the check engine light comes on. In life, the check engine light is only a warning which may appear as inconvenience, or it may be a discomfort which is really an indicator that something needed to be attended to. The breakdown is the tipping point. The warning unfortunately was overlooked and now life takes the steering wheel and changes you and your situation. It's our inability to respond correctly in a timely manner or the inactivity that allows this cycle to be the story of our lives. However, with the proper shift in our perspective, we can resume the control in our own lives in no time flat. I guess I should say, in no time flat, based on when and how you responded to the warning light on the engine.

Imagine that same check engine light came on, and the second you noticed it, you took it straight to the shop. What does the next few weeks of life look like for you? It is a possible inconvenience due to leaving in the hands of the mechanics, but great joy most likely because you caught whatever the problem was in time and was able to get ahead of a costly headache, or a costly repair? And you didn't need to experience being stranded on the side of the road in the middle of the night or in a place where help can't reach you.

The same is true in life. It's as if warning signs begin to pop up all over the place. You know the kind of signs like goose bumps appear on your skin. They are simply normal indicators that your body temperature is changing due to possibly an unexpected encounter with something or someone. Maybe there is a sudden change in the weather and you need to get to either a warmer place of better clothing. One thing is for sure. Something needs to be addressed.

If we learn to be proactive in life instead of reactive, we can get ahead of the curve and help to prevent the difficulties by learning the lessons. This is instead of experiencing the jolting effects of the tipping point. Therefore, all of our lessons tend to be hard. However, if you're tired of bumping your head then you have to learn when to duck. As my grandmother used to say "A hard head makes a soft behind"!

That being said, the first half of this book was changing the way we think and perceive life. The second half is about applying the new approach to life's experiences. It's about changing the walk. What does it mean to change the walk? In its simplest terms, it's the work that we have to do. It's building healthy habits, it's the day in- day out grind, and focusing on the change of behavior. Ask yourself, "What is it going to take for me to change? Does every progression have to have a tipping point? Or can I get ahead of that and began to coach my own growth?"

Change...The Inevitable
Christopher J. Taylor

That is the power of choice and the blessing in being a human being. We truly have unlimited potential and a society that for the most part is designed to give us opportunity. So, what are you going to do? Are you simply going to stand around, and perhaps feel sorry for yourself and complain about the situation at hand?

Or maybe, you'll learn all this information from life and tons of studying only to fail to use it appropriately. What good does it do for a person to be intelligent, and at the same time lack the power or the strength to utilize the intelligence? People of every ethnicity struggle with this in the worst of ways. We are without a doubt, creatures of habit. When we are young, the way we learn to do most things is the way we still do them in our older years.

This is about how we have learned to put together the puzzle pieces of life. Mankind's thinking, reasoning, and logic has flaws and the ability to correct them. Life is forever evolving. Therefore, our approach has to evolve as well. Nothing stays the same; everything is changing from the microscopic to macro. With that being said, we have to erase that old mentality. that reactive and lazy posture that we've sort of fell into, you know that old excuse if it isn't broke... don't fix it attitude. By the way that is backwards! Why in the world would anyone wait until something breaks to fix it when you can do maintenance and take preventive measures? We have to become forward thinkers thus curtailing bad results.

One thing we all can relate to is a weather forecast like a rainstorm or tornado. It's important to tune in and listen to the meteorologist. It's even wiser to invest in an umbrella even if it doesn't rain at least you're prepared. To think that it's a waste of time rather than to listen before preparing for what's down the road. It's this type of reaction that cripples growth, which allows us to become victims to our own vices, environments and circumstances. As long as we maintain this victim-like mentality things will always be happening to us and against us. We'll never be able to see our mistakes or accept the responsibilities in circumstance which in turn will never be resolved. It's so easy to blame everybody else. After all, it's not me at least that's what the world likes to think anyway. Isn't that how many people think?

In life, things are going to happen to all of us. Some are going to be out of our control. Often times, they are going to be unexpected events, situations and happenstances, and maybe even tragedies. That's just a part of this thing called "life". It is a universal law and no one is exempt from it. However, it's not what happens to us that defines us but how we respond. Even in the Bible, it speaks of a man being born of a few days that are filled with troubles. Remember, there is a purpose, lesson and a benefit in every hardship we endure. At the same time, if we fail to learn the lesson, not only will we forfeit the purpose and possibly lose the promotion, reward or benefits, but the painful situation will have been in vain and it undoubtedly will come again in a different shape, form, or fashion.

When we adapt the proactive mentality, we are essentially stepping into our rightful roles in this journey called life. You are the lead actor/actress in this movie! And I'm sorry being the supporting actor in my movie just doesn't cut it for me and it shouldn't work for you either. From this point on, in this very moment, you will begin to live a life of choice instead of a life of chance. Of course, it's bigger than choosing to wear a red shirt versus a green one. It's about choosing the right responses when faced with adversity.

Change...The Inevitable
Christopher J. Taylor

Yes...now we've hit the main artery of change, which is a simple six-lettered word called "choose." It's about choosing to coach growth at the first sign of discomfort instead of reacting at the moment of the tipping point. Life does not have to keep slapping you in the face every time it wants to get your attention. Or does it?

When the lesson is going to be a hard one, you'll be better off learning it once. If not, then the alternative will be long and a rough life full of unnecessary dramas which create headaches. It was said that time is your greatest commodity. You don't won't to waste your greatest commodity, "time", failing. It will be a habit of failing, repeat, reactivity, and victimization of your own life if you don't change the way your think. Never lose sight of your power of choice because it's yours and yours alone, you choose when you are mad, happy, discontent, or content.

Be careful of the company you keep, as they say, "Unwise associations eat up your harvest." Your life is like a seed in the soil of humanity. Your harvest is time, prosperity, money, life, etc. When you sense a test is approaching, start prepping yourself mentally to accept and analyze the situation, purpose and the process. Don't get hung up on the person, event or moment which is being skillfully used in the circumstance. This test is all about you and how you come through it. From it's in how you apply what you've learned that will determine whether or not you get to enjoy the fruit of your labor. Or you have to go through it all over again because you didn't understand process. Don't get caught up and let the moment blindside you. As they ole saying goes, "You can't see the forest for the trees." Every situation in life is a 'test.' Don't waste your time having to experience it again because you didn't learn the lesson it came to bring the first or second time.

Change...The Inevitable
Christopher J. Taylor

Most of all, remember that what we choose to do today paints the picture of our tomorrow.

Change...The Inevitable
Christopher J. Taylor

Chapter 7

Coaching Growth

"Always remember whatever you do in this life do it every day consistency is the key"

Ahmad Nelms

Communication rules the nation!

I remember being a young teenager, and having an argument with my Father about wanting to go to a party, and he just wouldn't allow me to go. I got upset and as soon as I was far enough to run just in case things went bad. I told him, "I can't wait till I'm grown so I can do what I want." He turned and looked at me. I thought it was about to go down so while I continued to get ready to run, he surprised me. He stared at me for a moment, and then calmly said, "One day you are going to wish you were a kid again." Then he turned and walked away. Under my breath I said," Yeah, right." That was one of the many things that I heard growing up. I also remember him saying, "You going to learn fat meat is greasy! Go ahead and say it...is fat meat greasy!" Now, if you ask me today if "fat meat is greasy", I will say unequivocally YES!

Every so often, I would ask him questions that he didn't feel like answering. And he would say "Just keep on living." I would like to take this time to say that he was right! In hindsight, particularly regarding my present situation in life and the situations of the countless men whose lives did not turn out right, we now know more than ever what you meant when you said "Just keep on living." So, as I look back, I understand that they were coming from a place of experience and love.

However, I wasn't able to understand exactly what those words and sayings really meant at that age, or in that young mental frame of mind. It's almost as if he was talking in riddles or parables to a person with a teenage comprehension. I just wasn't able to grasp the lesson that were enveloped in the phrases such as, "Trouble is easy to get into and hard to get out of", I mean, believe me, I got a very clear understanding now in hindsight. Twenty years ago, I had no idea what he was talking about. Twenty years later I know exactly what he was talking about. Oh, what a difference a day makes, right?

The beautiful thing about that story is there are a couple of valuable lessons in it. As I've grown over the years, I have reflected on my life and have tried to pinpoint some of those deciding moments and situations that played a role in the direction that my life has gone in.

One thing that stands out is how my father wasn't able to reach me using his approach, and for the longest I thought that I just wasn't able to be reached. Turns out, I was wrong, because there were people in the community that I listened to. Thinking back, I've learned that we all have a language. When it comes to effective communication, we must know the language of the person that we are trying to communicate. Especially, with the understanding that we are all different people from different walks of life. Hence, the way that we send and receive information differs as well.

Think about this. Have you ever met someone and for some inexplicable reason, you two just clicked almost to the point that you could finish their sentence or their thoughts? Author Gary Chapman, author of "The Five Love Languages," introduces us to five languages that people speak in relationships. The long and short of this powerful book is in all relationships you have to know how to reach a person by understanding their "language." In turn, you must learn your own language so that you may express the way you need to be cared for. Public speakers have to know their audience, especially when they are in the position to influence another person. As a mentor, the responsibility is on them to ensure that the message is being sent the right way and its through knowing how the person they're mentoring processes information that this done. The same has to be true for parenting. One form of discipline does not always work on different children, so one style of teaching, loving, and supporting must follow the same concept. The last thing a young mind needs is a life lesson wrapped in a riddle that can't be understood which ultimately doesn't do them any good. What happens is, once one of life's lessons is learned the hard way; the best an individual can do is exercise hindsight. However, if the message is presented in their language, the individual has a better chance of comprehending and making a well-informed choice. Think about your learning style are you an audio, visual, or tactile learner? Now, take a look at the people you influence (i.e. Children, students, siblings etc.) What are their learning styles? These are important questions to be answered within ourselves as well as others.

We have to become aware that the responsibility is on us! We owe it to the young men and women coming along the path of growth and maturity behind us, to layout the lesson we've learned in a clear and concise yet comprehensive manner. We can make the differences that we want to make on a broad scale if we learn how to communicate to one another. It's an important tool in coaching growth.

In history, we can see the development of civilizations which essentially are the results of some of the grand ideas of thinkers and inventors. Look at the greatest nations, and you can trace their success back to someone who was responsible for advancing that society. The goal has to be to build upon their success to stand upon the shoulders of others not reinvent their genius. That is how we as humans advance, we learn from those before us. We are coached, mentored, and in some cases, its pure grit and determination that propels ones' progress. My question to you is what propels yours?

What would you think if I told you I had the best idea in the world? I mean the million-dollar baby set for the rest of our lives type of idea, what would you say? You would probably say "I knew you were the one... brother." Then, when I told you that my idea was to re-invent the cell phone, you would probably burst out laughing, unfriend me and block me on all social media platforms! That's because we don't reinvent the wheel, we can enhance it!

The same is true when we talk about the lessons that we have learned in life. It doesn't make sense for the people who are following in our footsteps to make the same mistakes that we did. We should be offering our knowledge, experiences and advice to the next generation so that they might be able to build on our successes and learn to avoid failures and pitfalls. The same way we should be building on the experiences of the ones who came before us. We should be laying the bread crumbs for those coming behind. If you knew better, you would do better, right? Well, I'm banking that a lot of us already know better, so, what's the excuse? At the end of the day, LeBron James, Tom Brady, and Floyd Mayweather would not be the best in their respective fields had someone not took a vested interest in them. It's about being able to support and maximize a person's potential so that they may have a fair opportunity to walk in purpose.

Coaching growth doesn't stop there. We have to remember that life is forever evolving. That means that as much of an investment we have in the next generation, we have to be willing to invest in ourselves as well. The foundation of change in the vein of growth and development is about how to turn information into transformation. In other words, how do we take what we have learned and apply it?

We are all different people, no doubt. However, we are pretty much in pursuit of the same things, which are peace, love and happiness. How we get there is going to look very different for all of us. However, I promise you one thing. Your perspective is your reality, and the moment that you understand the way you have experienced this world thus far has created that very perspective. You'll understand that you have the choice in the direction you decide to take for your life. That being said what does your tomorrow look like? After all, it's your purpose that you're walking in.

Change...The Inevitable
Christopher J. Taylor

Chapter 8

Change

*"Change can be scary, but what's scarier is
allowing fear to stop you from growing, evolving
and progressing"*

Mandy Hale

As we continue on this journey towards living our best lives it's important to pay attention to how influential our mental view is in shaping our future. We have a general understanding of how we see, and perceive, which directly affects everything. And how we experience life at an early age can have a profound effect on the way we approach situations throughout adulthood. When we clean those lenses and remove the distortions and limitations, our vision will begin to focus. I have to warn you change is both inevitable and uncomfortable however it is a necessary part of this life journey.

Do you know about the life cycle of a caterpillar and its quest to become a butterfly? Looking through the lens of nature at the butterfly, whose wings are bursting with colors as they gently go through the motions of life, you would never have imagined the life it lived before transforming through its own self-weaved cocoon. It's even harder to realize this same beautiful graceful creature use to crawl along on the ground from one place to the other but now through its metamorphism it can fly ever so gently from one place to the other. Our lives are like that of the Butterfly. As we go through hard and uncomfortable times, we'll grow through them as well.

As you begin to weave you cocoon of transformation, you may start to grow apart from many relationships as well as outgrow some circumstances. Friends and family members will notice a difference in you, and they may say things to you regarding the changes they see. Some people will encourage you while others may "hate" and try to discourage, poking at the fact that you've changed. They'll be right, you will have changed, and things will be different. So, as you emerge from your cocoon as a Butterfly, beautiful wings spread wide, remember what's important. You are moving in the direction of your purpose as long as your changes are in the direction of positivity, growth and betterment you are on the right track.

The very idea of change is to make or become different and the mere thought or mention of the word change to many people is scary. However, some will see the power you reclaim over your life and they're going to want that for themselves. At the same time, some are going to fight this irrefutable law by couching their argument in the idea that you think you are too good to hang out with them when the truth will be quite the opposite. You will be in pursuit of your goals, of your best self, of living in and on purpose, your purpose and not theirs.

It's not going to be easy, this I assure you but at the end of the day you have to be the director and lead actor/ actress in this movie of life. You are the king on your chess board. You are the number one person in your life. People come into our lives for reasons and seasons. You must be wise enough to know both the reason they've come and the length of the season they'll stay. The important things to remember is when their season is up to let them go. Every new day will bring new opportunities, new interactions and experiences but it's with new eyes (perception) that you'll see and be in position to capitalize. Expect the very same people who didn't notice you before to suddenly start to look your way again. There is something undeniable about the aura or light that shines through a person who knows who they are, knows the power that they possess, and moves with specific intent and purpose.

When these new relationships begin to form, do not doubt their genuineness. It's okay to guard your heart. At the same time, you must guard against insecurities and skepticism because they are the very thinking distortions that we are working to wipe away from our consciousness. Learn to assess the people that are in your life with careful forethought. However, trust the process. Remember, that you are in the driver's seat, and people will always treat you how you allow them to. Everything in this world changes. Nothing stays the same. That is the nature of life. Your goal is to get behind your dreams. Turn them into visions, and make this life work for you.

One thing that I want to stress is that real change is forever! Just like there is no going back to yesterday, there will be no going back to the way we use to be. Butterflies don't turn back into caterpillars. Cats don't turn back into kittens, so you can't resort back into "the old you." We are talking about changing who we are. That means that our transformation is down to the core. The focus has never been on the behavior itself. It's been on the root causes of those behaviors. That being said, to simply change the way we act would do us a disservice. We must address our issues at the root, so that we can begin to produce better fruit.

Trees Vines and Weeds

When you think about trees, vines, and weeds, what comes to mind? Did you know that every seed must undergo the process in order to move on into its fruitful stages of life? That process usually takes place in a dark, wet hole, below soil. As we know, there are lessons in just about every aspect of life and nature. Those lessons depend on how you see things and how they resonate within your mind as a person.

Think about this. Imagine yourself standing in the forest for the sole purpose of comparing three kinds of plant life to the personalities of people. Trees, vines, and weeds at the seed level have are a lot of similarities. All three are small and are in a stagnant 'sleep' state. I mean, really nothing much going on in terms of growth as far as you can see. However, once they are planted in the rich soil of the forest and watered, they began to sprout. Even at this stage, it's hard to really see the difference between the tree, vine and the weed. They all are small, possibly green and fighting for sunlight. At the next stage, they began to take along their individual plantlike features and characteristics. It's here that you will be able to visibly see their differences. The aim is to get as much sunlight as possible and water however that's easier said than done. The weeks, months and even years come and go as these life forms mature as they reach for the rays of light from the Sun. The weed for example will probably grow faster than any other plant with the potential of spreading through the soil. Photosynthesis is the remarkable process of life that takes place beneath the delicate skin of each plant. Next, let's look at vine creeping along the ground or for that fact anything that it can adhere to searching for something sturdy to latch onto because it doesn't have the strong stock like a lot of plants have period its fault for sunlight depends on its ability to climb upwards by any means necessary. Seeing that the trees offered this tall structure or fences nearby, the Vine will climb as far as that tree or fence will allow. The tree on the other hand will grow upward to the top of the forest canopy searching and stretching and reaching for the very Rays of light that causes it to grow. The tree has strong roots, as well as a strong stalk, which enables it to hold itself up in weather the storms. As I think of trees, vines, and weeds as a person's perspective, I can't help but to think about the role that the soil plays in their ability to live and to grow.

Ask yourself, if you were one of these plants, which one would you prefer to be? Now, think of the soil as the environment, which requires you to determine whether it was rich in nutrients i.e., healthy with plenty of sunlight and water, which would make it perfect for growth? Or was it depleted, barren, and void of the necessary components of life thus causing you to be destructive? Is your current environment conducive or detrimental to your growth? Weeds are like those people whose lives have no real direction, no goals, no insight, and no purpose. Their perspective is small enough to put inside a box. In other words, they are immature, undeveloped, and self-centered. With that, they have no desire to attain more than what they want. They have a spirit of complacency that begins to form overhead about themselves. A glass ceiling that they can't seem to shatter and they can't break out of the prison of their mind. With that, they have no desire to team more than what they have period vines are like those people who want more in life, yet they don't have it in them to give up and put it into motion are the strength to focus and stay consistent therefore they latch onto the trees. They want the sunlight and would do anything to get it, so they ride on the backs of anyone headed to the top.

These people are not driven by purpose. They are driven by privileges. Then we have trees, a type of people that stand tall on their own. They grow to magnificent heights. Their roots are solid and strong from drinking life from the rich soil beneath. Soaking up vast amounts of sunlight drinking in water unlimited, while experiencing longevity in their lives, they understand focus direction insight strength energy. A level only other trees can understand.

I want to make it clear that these analogies are designed to represent human perspectives. The way that we see things and approach life, and not people themselves. There are stages of growth. Unfortunately, not everyone will mature from one stage to another. However, my hope is that everyone has at least the opportunity and understands their power thus becoming equipped with the tools to make the necessary changes in their lives.

We have all been through our hard times some of us were born into them while others experienced them later in life. When they happened doesn't matter. What's important is that we are able to understand how they have affected the way we see life which is our perception. Knowing yourself is of the utmost importance, and when it comes to this journey called, it is your life not just in your development immaturity but in this pursuit of wholeness.

History is the biggest gift that we could ask for in this regard. It's a privilege to have someone else successes and failures, laid out before you with the sole purpose of empowering and enlightening one's path. It's an opportunity to learn from their lessons and build upon their advancements. History, more importantly your history, is a window into the past. This is a past that has created your today and offers you a template for changing your tomorrow. You just have to be willing to put in the work.

Change is, well it's a lot of things. However, one thing we can agree on is it's inevitable. It's going to happen. Therefore, let's stop resisting that which is natural and let's start to write our own story. A story where you are the star! Where you control the narrative !

Goal Setting Strategy

It's important to have a plan of action. A well thought out strategy will enable you to measure and monitor progress as well as help to avoid unnecessary pitfalls. Remember, when you don't have a plan, you ultimately plan to fail.

Options to consider: Is the goal purposeful? Is it attainable? Is it realistic?

Step 1: Clearly defined the goal.

Step 2: Break the goal down into five easily achievable steps. Writing these steps out on paper or creating a vision board has proven helpful.

Step 3: Make a detailed list of all the resources you need to complete each task

Step 4: Work application is key when achieving any goal. If you can develop a strong work ethic and move with a purpose the odds of success are in your favor.

Step 5: Plan to expand. When reaching goals rooted in purpose, the accomplishment of one goal will land you at the base of another. That being said every individual plan should interconnect, moving you toward your big picture, your final accomplishment, the grandmaster of purpose.

About the author:

Christopher Joseph Alfred Taylor is an aspiring author and journalist. He is serving a life sentence in Colorado's Department of Correction where he is currently working as an Offender Care Aid Ill. In his free time, he mentors his peers in one-on-one settings as well as through motivational presentations. Using his life as an example, he has created the C.A.T.C.H. Project (Changing Attitudes through Cognitive Healing). A class aimed at the cognitive development of at-risk youth. He's also co-facilitator of the S.U.R.G.E. movement, as well as, editor and contributor to the Resource Newsletter.

About the Book

In these pages of Change …The inevitable is an invitation to a deeper understanding of self. Come journey with me as we attempt to connect the dots between past experiences, present day perspectives, and future desires. This book offers relatable examples as well as practical techniques and exercises all designed to encourage and empower you. If you are fed up with the cycle of unhealthy relationships, tired of the same patterns of behavior, or are just simply looking for some tools that may help inspire growth, this is the book that you've been waiting for. This is a must read! Ten percent of each book sold will be donated to non-profit organizations in honor of Krystal Martinez, Kyle Boyd, and Susan Holifield.

Contact Christopher at:

Christopher J.A. Taylor Reg# 133875

Po Box 392004

Denver, Co. 80239

Or by email:

catchonesaveone@gmail.com

Quotes

1. "Life will only change when you become more committed to your dreams than you are to your comfort zones." - Anonymous.

2. "Change can be scary, but what's scarier is allowing fear to stop you from growing, evolving and progressing" - Mandy Hale

3. "Working hard for something we don't care about is called stress, working hard for something we love is called passion" - Anonymous

4. "The best way to predict the future is to create it" - Peter Drucker

5. "Greatness begins beyond your comfort zone" - Robin Sharma

6. "Do something uncomfortable today by stepping out of your box. You don't have to settle for what you are- you get to create who you want to become" - Howard Walstein

7. "Every positive change in life begins with a clear unequivocal decision that you're going to either do something or stop doing something"- Anonymous

8. "Carefully watch your thoughts, for they become words. Manage and watch your words, for they become your actions. Consider and judge your actions, for they have become your habits. Acknowledge and watch your habits, for they should become your values. Understand and embrace your values for they become your destiny" - Mahatma Gandhi

• "Pain is never wasted" - Francine Segura

• "There are lessons and blessings in everything that we go through"- Christopher J Taylor

• "Every person must eat from the garden that they have planted" - Travis Barnes

• "You shouldn't have the luxury of being bored" - William S. Graham

• "Always remember whatever you do in this life do it every day consistency is the key"- Ahmad Nelms

• "You eat what you kill meaning your accomplishments are only the evidence of the work you put in" - Rory Atkins